STATISTICS WITH A SENSE OF HUMOR

A Humorous Workbook
and
Guide to Study Skills

Fred Pyrczak
California State University, Los Angeles

Pyrczak Publishing
P.O. Box 39731
Los Angeles, CA 90039
(213) 660-7600

Statistical Consultant: Robert Morman

Editors: Deborah Finkel and Linda Sasser

Design: Robin McBurney

ISBN 0-9623744-0-7

INTRODUCTION

Hello, I'm Dr. P.

Welcome to the world of statistics. You will be acquiring skills used in many fields of investigation.

Statistics is different from many other courses you may have taken:

(1) It has an extensive technical vocabulary that must be mastered.

(2) The course is highly cumulative. Many of the things you learn will be referred to again and again throughout the course in various contexts. Failure to master concepts and procedures early in the course will cause serious problems later.

(3) Statistics is a precise field. A seemingly minor mistake in procedures may lead to a very wrong answer.

What this all adds up to is NOT that statistics should be dreaded--heavens no! Instead, it means that in order to derive the maximum benefit from this important course and feel comfortable at the same time, you must consistently apply the very best study skills.

I have collected dozens of study skill techniques from the research literature and recast them to help you with your study of statistics.

To get the maximum benefit from my advice, read all of the essays on study skills, which are interspersed among the worksheets, *during the first week of the semester.* Much of my advice can and should be followed right from the beginning of the course. Review the essays when you come to them again while completing the worksheets. In each essay, there is a place for you to respond in writing. Be sure to take a few minutes to respond to each one.

All of you will find this workbook useful because it will give you the practice in computations needed to build the confidence and speed you will need while taking tests in statistics. It will help whether you are using a calculator or computer.

For those of you whose math skills are a bit rusty, the first six worksheets will help you review basic math used in statistics.

If you are somewhat anxious, you will find friendly tips in this book that will help you. Also, the humorous riddles will provide comic relief when the going gets rough.

Some worksheets cover basic concepts in statistics. These are not comprehensive; your instructor will probably expect you to know much more. The study skills you will learn here, however, will provide you with the skills you need to master additional concepts presented in both lectures and your textbook.

I would wish you good luck, but luck is not the key to success in statistics. Instead, I wish you hard work, persistence, and good study skills.

Fred Pyrczak
Los Angeles, California

Notes on Computations and Rounding on Worksheets:

The directions on most worksheets indicate the number of decimal places to report in your answers. Solve to one more decimal place than requested in the directions. For example, if the directions state, "Round your answers to two decimal places," solve to three decimal places and round to two.

Some statistical formulas require several steps. The answers given in this workbook were obtained by rounding at each step to one more decimal place than required in the final answer. For example, if an answer to two decimal places is required for a two-step problem, the answer to the first step should be rounded to three decimal places from the fourth. The answer to the second and final step should be rounded from three to two.

When computing answers, fractions were converted to their decimal equivalents as soon as permitted under the rules of mathematics.

The special rule for rounding off numbers ending in five (5), described on Worksheet 3, should be followed whenever applicable throughout this workbook.

If you use alternative computational procedures--such as allowing the number of decimal places to float in your calculator--*you may need to make allowances when checking your answers*. Some of your answers may occasionally differ in the tenth's place and beyond.

TABLE OF CONTENTS

Worksheets

Study Skills

NOTES:

Dr. P.'s friendly advice: PLEASE DON'T IGNORE THE INTRODUCTION TO THIS BOOK.

    If you don't read it, (1) you won't know why statistics is different from many other courses you've taken, (2) you won't know what this book will and will not do for you, and (3) you won't know when you should first read all of the essays on study skills in this book.
    When should you first read all the essays?

(P.S. Have you read the introduction to your textbook yet?)

Name: _____ Date: _____

Worksheet 1: MATH REVIEW: ORDER OF OPERATIONS

RIDDLE: Why did the bored man cut a hole in the carpet?

Directions: To find the answer to the riddle, write the answers to the problems on the lines. The letter in the solution section beside the answer to the first problem is the first letter in the answer to the riddle, the letter beside the answer to the second problem is the second letter, and so on.

1. 5 x 10 + 6 x 2 = _____

2. 3 + 4 x 9 = _____

3. (9 + 28) x 6 = _____

4. 159 - 66 x 2 = _____

5. 15 x 14 - 8 x 20 = _____

6. 19 - 5 + 2 x 3 = _____

7. 70 - 5 x 3 x 4 = _____

8. 6 + 8 x 1 x 5 = _____

9. 33/1 + 1 x 3 = _____

10. 8/4 + (6)(0) = _____

11. 169/(12 + 1) = _____

12. (2 + 3 + 4)/3 = _____

13. (2 + 18)/(9 - 5) = _____

14. (1 + 5)(3) + (7)(2) = _____

15. (9 + 9)(10 - 1)(2) = _____

16. (15 - 4)(21/7)(63-59) = _____

17. (3)(1)(1) + (6/2)(9) = _____

SOLUTION SECTION:

112 (B)	62 (T)	39 (O)	10 (H)	780 (Y)	222 (S)	3 (O)
2 (L)	63 (A)	27 (E)	177 (Z)	186 (X)	13 (O)	5 (R)
32 (S)	50 (E)	4,040 (D)	20 (T)	46 (E)	30 (W)	70 (F)
132 (O)	102 (K)	36 (F)	324 (H)	187 (B)	1 (J)	48 (I)

Write the answer to the riddle here, putting one letter on each line:

____ ____   ____ ____ ____   ____ ____ ____

____ ____ ____ ____ ____   ____ ____ ____ ____

Dr. P.'s friendly advice: CALCULATOR TIPS:

1. Don't become overconfident because you are using a calculator. Many students who use calculators make as many mistakes as those who calculate using only pencil and paper.

2. Using a calculator doesn't relieve you of the responsibility to do all problems twice. It's the best way to check your work.

3. Be sure to read the directions for your calculator thoroughly and carefully. You need to understand the functions of all keys. At the very least, perform all the sample problems in the calculator's manual.

   If you haven't read the directions for your calculator yet, read them now and write two new things you learned about it. (For very simple calculators, you may only learn how to change the battery--but you need even that information.)

1. _____

2. _____

Name: _____   Date: _____

Worksheet 2: MATH REVIEW: NEGATIVES

RIDDLE: What did the owner of the wreck of a car say about the noise it makes?

Directions: To find the answer to the riddle, write the answers to the problems on the lines. The word in the solution section beside the answer to the first problem is the first word in the answer to the riddle, the word beside the answer to the second problem is the second word, and so on.

1. $(-10)(-2) =$ _____

2. $(-5)(47) =$ _____

3. $(6)(-16) =$ _____

4. $15/-3 =$ _____

5. $-144/12 =$ _____

6. $-169/-13 =$ _____

7. $19 + -3 =$ _____

8. $-28 + -28 =$ _____

9. $-88 + 18 =$ _____

10. $15 - -15 =$ _____

11. $-29 - 14 =$ _____

12. $-30 - -29 =$ _____

13. $(-15)(-33) =$ _____

14. $(-11)(44) =$ _____

15. $-2178/33 =$ _____

16. $188 + -99 =$ _____

17. $-279 + -188 =$ _____

18. $-399 - 59 =$ _____

SOLUTION SECTION:

-20 (GARAGE)   235 (TWO)   340 (SKY)   20 (THERE'S)   -96 (ONE)

-235 (ONLY)   96 (ROAD)   -56 (THAT)   -70 (DOESN'T)   -1 (SORT)

-458 (HORN)   -467 (THE)   5 (IS)   -12 (ON)   -5 (THING)   13 (MY)

-13 (USE)   16 (CAR)   12 (BE)   30 (MAKE)   0 (FIX)   22 (BUS)

495 (OF)   -484 (NOISE)   56 (AN)   -66 (AND)   70 (TRANSPORTATION)

89 (THAT'S)   -43 (SOME)   -15 (ALWAYS)   -59 (HIGHWAY)

-495 (MECHANIC)   66 (BROKEN)   484 (STRANDED)   467 (FREEWAY)

Write the answer to the riddle here, putting one word on each line:

_____ _____ _____ _____ _____ _____

_____ _____ _____ _____ _____ _____

_____ _____ _____ _____ _____

NOTES:

Dr. P.'s friendly advice: MAKE MENTAL ESTIMATES OF THE ANSWERS TO CALCULATIONS.

Successful students in statistics usually make mental estimates of answers even if they are using a calculator or computer. Then, if the answer given by the calculator or computer is not close to the estimate, they know a mistake has occurred.

Suppose you need to multiply the two numbers shown above. One way to estimate the answer is to round each to the nearest whole number and multiply mentally. What is your estimate? _____   The answer you get on your calculator should be close to this.

Another way to estimate is to round both numbers up. By doing so and then multiplying, what estimate do you get? _____ Because both were rounded up, you know that the answer on your calculator must be somewhat LESS than your estimate if it is correct.

At first, making mental estimates may slow you down a bit, but in the long run you'll save time and make fewer errors.

Name: _____ Date: _____

Worksheet 3: MATH REVIEW: ROUNDING

RIDDLE: What did the psychologist put on a sign in her office to make her patients pay?

Directions: To find the answer to the riddle, write the answers to the problems on the lines. The word in the solution section beside the answer to the first problem is the first word in the answer to the riddle, the word beside the answer to the second problem is the second word, and so on.

Round as usual except when rounding off a number ending in a five (5). If the number immediately preceding a five is odd, round up. If the number immediately preceding a five is even, round down. Another way to state this principle is: "round to the nearest even number all numbers ending in 5." For example, 4.85 rounds to 4.8; 4.75 rounds to 4.8. Notice, however, that 4.851, which ends in a value greater than "5," rounds to 4.9.

1. Round 10.543 to the nearest hundredth: _____

2. Round 8.67 to the nearest tenth: _____

3. Round 8.4 to the nearest whole number: _____

4. Round 9.8452 to the nearest thousandth: _____

5. Round 15.839 to the nearest tenth: _____

6. Round 29.5 to the nearest whole number: _____

7. Round 15.86 to the nearest tenth: _____

8. Round 3.945 to the nearest hundredth: _____

9. Round 8.45 to the nearest tenth: _____

10   Round 10.555555 to the nearest hundredth: _____

SOLUTION SECTION:

29 (CRAZY)   15.9 (THE)   8.7 (THE)   30 (PAY)   3.95 (AM)   8 (AMNESIA)

10.56 (ADVANCE)   8.4 (IN)   8.5 (ONLY)   3.94 (PSYCHOLOGIST)   15.8 (MUST)

9845 (IS)   15.4 (BILL)   9.85 (HELPS)   9.846 (NEVER)   10 (LOVING)

9.845 (PATIENTS)   9 (LIFE)   10.54 (ALL)   10.5 (COUNSELING)   4 (DISTURBED)

Write the answer to the riddle here, putting one word on each line:

_____   _____   _____   _____   _____   _____

_____   _____   _____

NOTES:

Dr. P.'s friendly advice: FORM A CIRCLE OF FRIENDS IN STATISTICS.

Here's how:
Pass around a sheet of paper on which students can write their names and phone numbers. Those who wish to participate can call each other when they have a problem.
This will give you a larger circle of people to contact if your study group can't help you with a problem.
Associate the names on the list with the faces in class. It will make you more comfortable when you call someone or someone calls you. List the names of four students below. Try to associate their names with their faces during your next class meeting.

_____   _____

_____   _____

Name: _____   Date: _____

Worksheet 4: MATH REVIEW: DECIMALS

RIDDLE: What did the bore do to help the party?

Directions: To find the answer to the riddle, write the answers to the problems on the lines. The letter in the solution section beside the answer to the first problem is the first letter in the answer to the riddle, the letter beside the answer to the second problem is the second letter, and so on.
      If an answer has more than two decimal places, round to two.

1. 0.02 multiplied by 1 = _____

2. 1.1 multiplied by 1.11 = _____

3. 5.999 multiplied by 0 = _____

4. 3.77 multiplied by 4.69 = _____

5. 12.4 divided into 169.38 = _____

6. 15.9 divided by 1 = _____

7. 12.1 plus 99.98 = _____

8. 3.11 plus 8.99 = _____

9. 18.3 subtracted from 25.46 = _____

10. 10.01 minus 8.873 = _____

SOLUTION SECTION:

1.22 (E)	0.2 (C)	0.14 (X)	7.16 (M)	71.6 (D)	0 (W)
6.00 (K)	2.11 (F)	0.02 (H)	112.08 (H)	101.19 (P)	
15.9 (T)	1.59 (B)	13.66 (N)	1.21 (J)	17.68 (E)	
1.366 (G)	12.10 (O)	0.177 (R)	1.14 (E)	1.111 (S)	

Write the answer to the riddle here, putting one letter on each line:

____ ____   ____ ____ ____ ____   ____ ____ ____ ____

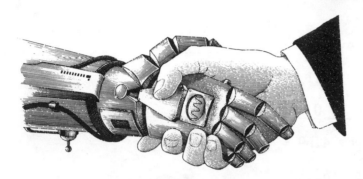

Dr. P.'s friendly advice: YOU'RE MEETING THE FUTURE IN STATISTICS!

All professional fields are relying increasingly on statistics, and this trend should continue into the future.

Here are some examples of how they are being used:

Medicine: Determine reliability of differences between experimental drugs and placebos.

Business: Project future sales based on past trends.

Education: Plan new school facilities using statistics on population trends.

Name the professional field for which you are preparing:

_____

Name one or two ways statistics are used in your field:

_____

_____

Share your answers with your classmates.

Name: _____ Date: _____

Worksheet 5: MATH REVIEW: FRACTIONS AND DECIMALS

RIDDLE: Why should you respect the lily?

Directions: To find the answer to the riddle, write the answers to the problems on the lines. The word in the solution section beside the answer to the first problem is the first word in the answer to the riddle, the word beside the answer to the second problem is the second word, and so on. Express fractions in lowest terms.

1. $1/5 + 3/5 =$ _____   5. $2/3 \times 2/3 =$ _____

2. $1/5 + 1/10 =$ _____   6. $2/5 \times 4/7 =$ _____

3. $3/9 - 1/9 =$ _____   7. $2/9$ divided by $1/9 =$ _____

4. $1 - 7/8 =$ _____   8. 5 divided into $2/3 =$ _____

9.   What is the decimal equivalent of $1/2$? = _____

10. What is the decimal equivalent of $3/4$? = _____

11. What is the decimal equivalent of 2 and $2/3$? = _____

12. What is the decimal equivalent of 2 and $3/4$? = _____

13. What is the decimal equivalent of 2 and $1/10$? = _____

14. What fraction corresponds to 0.2? = _____

15. What fraction corresponds to 0.11? = _____

16. What fraction corresponds to 0.555? = _____

SOLUTION SECTION:

4/5 (NEVER)   2/5 (SEE)   3/10 (LOOK)   11/20 (IS)   0.5 (DAY)

0.55 (FLOWERS)   2/3 (FLORIST)   4/9 (A)   2/9 (DOWN)   2.1 (LOOK)

1/5 (DOWN)   11/100 (ON)   2/35 (CLEAN)   8/35 (LILY)   1/8 (ON)

2/81 (HOPE)   2 (BECAUSE)   2/15 (ONE)   0.75 (A)   2.67 (LILY)

2.75 (WILL)   111/200 (YOU)   8/8 (EASTER)   3 1/3 (BEAUTIFUL)

Write the answer to the riddle here, putting one word on each line:

_____ _____ _____ _____ _____ _____ _____ _____

_____ _____ _____ _____ _____ _____ _____ _____

NOTES:

Dr. P.'s friendly advice: THREE HEADS ARE BETTER THAN ONE!

  Form a study group with at least three members. With three, you'll have a member to work with even if someone misses a study session or if (HEAVEN FORBID!) a member drops the course.

  Don't hesitate to take a student who is struggling with statistics into your group. This could be a valuable learning experience for you. As you explain concepts and procedures, your own skills will become sharper. (*P.S.* You'll also feel good for helping someone who will appreciate your assistance.)

  Write the names and phone numbers of your study group members here:

_____

_____

_____

When you get home, copy these into your phone book.

Name: _____ Date: _____

Worksheet 6: MATH REVIEW: ALGEBRAIC MANIPULATIONS

RIDDLE: When do actors and actresses get stage fright?

Directions: To find the answer to the riddle, write "T" for "true" or "F" for "false" on the line to the left of each statement. The word at the end of the first true statement is the first word in the answer to the riddle, the word at the end of the second true statement is the second word, and so on.

All variables are distinct from one another; that is, no variable equals any other variable.

_____ 1. If $A = C/D$, then $C = (A)(D)$ (WHEN)

_____ 2. If $A = C/D$, then $D = C/A$ (THEY)

_____ 3. If $P/B = F$, then $P = F/B$ (GET)

_____ 4. If $X + Y = 10$, then $X = 10 - Y$ (SEE)

_____ 5. If $25 = A + B$, then $A = 25 - B$ (AN)

_____ 6. If $X + 25 = W$, then $X = W + 25$ (CURTAIN)

_____ 7. If $A = C - D$, then $D = C + A$ (APPLAUSE)

_____ 8. If $A - D = F$, then $A = F + D$ (EGG)

_____ 9. If $A = F - G - H$, then $F = A - G - H$ (STAGE)

_____ 10. If $(B)(C) = P$, then $B = P/C$ (OR)

_____ 11. If $Y = (B)(F)$, then $B = F/Y$ (SCRIPT)

_____ 12. If $X = (N)(B)(C)$, then $B = X/(N)(C)$ (A)

_____ 13. If $X + Y = B - C$, then $B = X + (Y)(C)$ (VOICE)

_____ 14. If $(B)(Y) = (X)(C)$, then $C = (B)(Y)/X$ (TOMATO)

Write the answer to the riddle here, putting one word on each line:

_____ _____ _____ _____ _____ _____

_____ _____

NOTES:

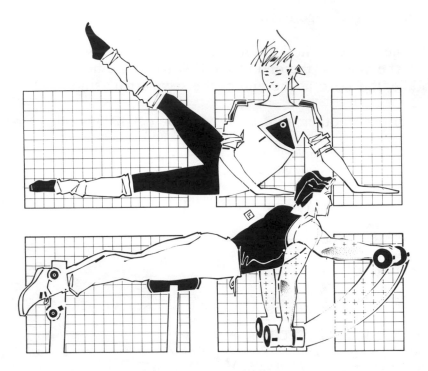

Dr. P.'s friendly advice: DO YOUR WORKOUT IN STATISTICS ON GRAPH PAPER.

Graph paper will help you keep all of your statistics work neatly organized in rows and columns.

If you're working with a formula that requires a number of computations, the columns on your graph paper will make it easier to spot a mistake caused by forgetting to bring down a term or value for use in later stages of your calculations.

Neatness is more than just a virtue in statistics. It's essential if you want to get right answers consistently.

What kind of paper did you last use when you computed an answer?

_____

If your answer is lined or blank paper, give graph paper a try. After you have used it for several hours, write your personal evaluation of this advice. Did it help you? Was your work neater and easier to follow? Why?

_____

_____

Name: _____ Date: _____

Worksheet 7: FREQUENCY DISTRIBUTION AND CUMULATIVE FREQUENCIES

RIDDLE: What is in the "honeymoon salad?"

Directions: First construct a frequency distribution on a separate piece of paper using an interval size of three (3) for the scores shown below. Also construct a column showing the percents (rounded to the nearest tenth) that correspond to the frequencies. To obtain the percents, divide the total number of cases into each frequency and multiply by 100. Then construct a column showing the cumulative frequencies.

　　　To find the answer to the riddle, write the answers to the problems on the lines. The word in the solution section beside the answer to the first problem is the first word in the answer to the riddle, the word beside the answer to the second problem is the second word, and so on.

SCORES:

16, 29, 15, 5, 3, 43, 20, 22, 4, 20, 22, 7, 8, 33,

8, 33, 15, 18, 10, 30, 44, 42, 40, 36, 25, 26, 21, 22,

12, 22, 28, 29, 31, 18, 20, 25, 40, 22, 27, 28, 30, 35,

6, 10, 22, 35, 39, 35, 22, 26, 32, 35, 38, 30, 26, 24

1. What is the frequency in the bottom interval? _____

2. What percent is in the interval from 21 to 23? _____

3. What percent is in the interval from 30 to 32? _____

4. What is the cumulative frequency in the top interval? _____
　　(Hint: The cf in the top interval always equals the total N.)

5. What is the cumulative frequency in the interval from 9 to 11? _____

SOLUTION SECTION:

2 (TOMATOES)　　　3.9 (CARROTS)　　　53 (DICED)　　　50 (HELPING)　　　7 (IS)

3 (LETTUCE)　　58 (RUSSIAN)　　　9 (DRESSING)　　　14.3 (ALONE)　　　4 (EAT)

8.9 (WITH)　　　10.7 (PLATE)　　　18 (FORK)　　　56 (NO)　　　7.1 (SOUR)

18 (TABLE)　　　6 (WAITER)　　　5 (KNIFE)　　　13 (BLUE)　　　15 (CHEESE)

Write the answer to the riddle here, putting one word on each line:

_____ _____ _____ _____ _____

NOTES:

Dr. P.'s friendly advice: A TUTOR MAY BE THE ANSWER TO YOUR PRAYERS!

If you find that you are having serious difficulties, get a tutor right away. Statistics is cumulative! What you don't learn in one chapter will likely show up again in a different context in a later chapter to haunt you. Schedule regular meetings each week with your tutor. Two or three shorter sessions a week are better than one very long one. Ask your tutor to give you some practice problems at the end of each session for you to work on independently. Also, ask your tutor to explain how to interpret each statistic you cover.

If you need a tutor, ask your instructor to suggest some sources of tutorial help and write the information here or in your notebook:

_____

_____

Name: _____   Date: _____

Worksheet 8: POLYGON

RIDDLE: What time is it when the clock strikes 13?

Directions: Convert the frequencies to percents and plot the percents with the corresponding midpoints of the intervals on graph paper. Use a solid line for School A and a dashed line for School B. Make each curve begin and end at zero percent by plotting the midpoints of one interval above and one interval below those shown on this page.
    To find the answer to the riddle, write "T" for "true" or "F" for "false" on the line to the left of each statement. The word at the end of the first true statement is the first word in the answer to the riddle, the word at the end of the second true statement is the second word, and so on.

X	School A f	P	School B f	P
39-41	1		5	
36-38	0		20	
33-35	4		0	
30-32	10		50	
27-29	15		75	
24-26	16		80	
21-23	11		50	
18-20	10		55	
15-17	8		60	
12-14	8		40	
9-11	12		40	
6-8	5		25	
	N =		N =	

_____ 1.   The dashed line drops to the base line (x axis) at a score of 34.
          (TIME)

CONTINUED

_____ 2. The solid line drops to the base line at a score of 34. (IT'S)

_____ 3. The dashed line drops to the base line at a score of 4. (TO)

_____ 4. The dashed line drops to the base line at a score of 40. (WATCH)

_____ 5. The solid line reaches its highest point at a score of 25. (THROW)

_____ 6. The solid line drops to the base line at a score of 37. (IT)

_____ 7. The dashed line reaches its highest point at a score of 16.
         (ALARM)

_____ 8. School B has a higher percent in the 9-11 interval than School A
         has. (FIX)

_____ 9. School B has a higher percent in the 27-29 interval than School A
         has. (LATE)

_____ 10. The dashed line reaches its highest point at a score of 37. (HANDS)

_____ 11. School A has a higher percent in the 33-35 interval than School B
          has. (AWAY)

Write the answer to the riddle here, putting one word on each line:

_____ _____ _____ _____ _____

Name: _____ Date: _____

Worksheet 9: THREE AVERAGES: COMPUTATIONS

RIDDLE: What's the difference between a poor man and a feather bed?

Directions: To find the answer to the riddle, write the answers to the problems on the lines. The word in the solution section beside the answer to the first problem is the first word in the answer to the riddle, the word beside the answer to the second problem is the second word, and so on.

Report your answers to two decimal places.

Group A's Scores: 12, 15, 7, 10, 5, 16, 7, 14

Group B's Scores: 16, 6, 10, 6, 16, 6, 15, 19, 23

1. What is the mean of Group A's scores? _____

2. What is the median of Group A's scores? _____

3. What is the mode of Group A's scores? _____

4. What is the mean of Group B's scores? _____

5. What is the median of Group B's scores? _____

6. What is the mode of Group B's scores? _____

7. What is the difference between the two means? _____

8. What is the difference between the two medians? _____

9. What is the difference between the two modes? _____

SOLUTION SECTION:

12.00 (POOR)	10.00 (MONEY)	11.00 (IS)	6.00 (OTHER)
7.00 (HARD)	16.00 (SLEEP)	13.00 (UP)	1.00 (DOWN)
5.00 (BEDROOM)	4.00 (SOFT)	3.00 (CLEAN)	10.75 (ONE)
15.00 (THE)	4.25 (AM)	2.25 (IS)	14.62 (HELPS)

Write the answer to the riddle here, putting one word on each line:

_____ _____ _____ _____ ; _____ _____

_____ _____ _____

NOTES:

Dr. P.'s friendly advice: STUDY CARDS WORK!

A highly effective technique is to develop study cards. On the front, write a problem or a statistical term. On the back, write the solution or definition.

It is especially important that you master statistical terms. Your instructor will be using them throughout the semester.

Make study cards even for concepts and skills that you feel comfortable with now. In a few months when you are preparing for the final exam, you will need to review everything.

P.S. What goes on the back of the card shown above?

_____

Name: _____   Date: _____

Worksheet 10: MEDIANS FROM FREQUENCY DISTRIBUTIONS

RIDDLE: Why did the muffler repair person quit her job?

Directions: To find the answer to the riddle, write the answers to the problems on the lines. The word in the solution section beside the answer to the first problem is the first word in the answer to the riddle, the word beside the answer to the second problem is the second word, and so on. Round your answers to two decimal places.

GROUP A			GROUP B			GROUP C	
X	f		X	f		X	f
19	7		100	20		600	2
18	8		99	55		599	0
17	10		98	68		598	3
16	5		97	47		597	7
15	3		96	21		596	4
			95	10		595	0
						594	5

GROUP D			GROUP E			GROUP F	
X	f		X	f		X	f
33–35	2		69–71	15		75–79	3
30–32	3		66–68	20		70–74	0
27–29	6		63–65	27		65–69	5
24–26	9		60–62	32		60–64	19
21–23	12		57–59	44		55–59	20
18–20	10		54–56	33		50–54	21
15–17	9		51–53	25		45–49	17
12–14	7		48–50	20		40–44	14
9–11	5		45–47	15		35–39	10
6–8	0		42–44	11		30–34	6
3–5	1		39–41	5		25–29	4
						20–24	1	CONTINUED

Worksheet 10: Continued

1. What is the median of Group A's scores? _____

2. What is the median of Group B's scores? _____

3. What is the median of Group C's scores? _____

4. What is the median of Group D's scores? _____

5. What is the median of Group E's scores? _____

6. What is the median of Group F's scores? _____

SOLUTION SECTION:

20.50 (HOME)   17.85 (PAY)   17.35 (SHE)   98.02 (WORKS)

57.49 (FEELING)   56.83 (AUTOMOBILES)   51.40 (EXHAUSTED)

49.88 (REPAIRS)   97.98 (ALWAYS)   7.21 (EMPLOYMENT)

596.71 (WENT)   18.5 (APPLICATION)   50.12 (DISCRIMINATION)

Write the answer to the riddle here, putting one word on each line:

_____ _____ _____ _____ _____ _____

Name: _____   Date: _____

Worksheet 11: AVERAGING MEANS

RIDDLE: What do you call a swine in the rain?

Directions: To find the answer to the riddle, write the answers to the problems on the lines. The letter in the solution section beside the answer to the first problem is the first letter in the answer to the riddle, the letter beside the answer to the second problem is the second letter, and so on.

    For each problem, calculate the precise mean of the means by first computing the sum of X for each group by multiplying M times N. Round your answers to one decimal place.

1. If $M = 50.00$ ($N = 10$) for Group A and $M = 100.00$ ($N = 30$) for Group B, what is the mean of the means? _____

2. If $M = 5.00$ ($N = 20$) for Group X and $M = 10.00$ ($N = 50$) for Group Y, what is the mean of the means? _____

3. If $M = 49.20$ ($N = 55$) for Group F and $M = 62.50$ ($N = 12$) for group D, what is the mean of the means? _____

4. If $M = 500.00$ ($N = 100$) for Group Z and $M = 400.00$ ($N = 200$) for Group T, what is the mean of the means? _____

5. If $M = 449.23$ ($N = 66$) for Group H and $M = 400.15$ ($N = 10$) for Group J, what is the mean of the means? _____

6. If $M = 21.52$ ($N = 24$) for Group P, $M = 30.66$ ($N = 33$) for Group Q, and $M = 39.87$ ($N = 500$) for Group R, what is the mean of the means? _____

7. If $M = 55.22$ ($N = 10$) for Group K and $M = 66.55$ ($N = 10$) for Group L, what is the mean of the means? _____

SOLUTION SECTION:

51.6 (G)	75.0 (B)	7.5 (E)	15.0 (K)	450.0 (N)
30.7 (Y)	60.9 (H)	38.5 (S)	87.5 (H)	55.8 (M)
433.3 (W)	442.8 (A)	424.7 (I)	8.6 (O)	

Write the answer to the riddle here, putting one letter on each line:

____ ____ ____ ____ ____ ____ ____

NOTES:

Dr. P.'s friendly advice: STUMPED BY A FORMULA? NOT GETTING THE RIGHT ANSWER?

Here are three effective things to do:

1. Check to see that you have copied the formula exactly as it is shown in your book. A seemingly slight change in the position of a symbol or a missing symbol can make a BIG difference in the answer.

2. Review the textbook example. Check to see where the numerical values that were substituted for symbols came from. For example, did you put the sum of the first column of scores in the same position in the formula as your author did?

3. If you are using a computer, review the data you have entered. A single incorrect entry may be the source of your problem.

During the next week or two, tally below the number of times each of the above is the source of your problems. Being aware of the sources of your errors will make you more alert to them in the future.

1. Did not copy formula correctly: _____

2. Entered data in incorrect position: _____

3. Entered incorrect data into program: _____

Name: _____   Name: _____

Worksheet 12: AVERAGES: CONCEPTS

RIDDLE: Why did the Idaho potato leave the United States?

Directions: To find the answer to the riddle, write "T" for "true" or "F" for "false" on the line to the left of each statement. The letter at the end of the first true statement is the first letter in the answer to the riddle, the letter at the end of the second true statement is the second letter, and so on.

_____ 1. The mean is the most frequently used average. (F)

_____ 2. Averages are sometimes called "measures of central tendency. " (R)

_____ 3. In a distribution with a positive skew, the median has a higher value than the mean. (A)

_____ 4. In a normal distribution, the mean, median and mode have the same value. (E)

_____ 5. The median has 50% of the cases below it ONLY in a normal distribution. (I)

_____ 6. The mean has 50% of the cases below it regardless of the shape of the distribution. (T)

_____ 7. The mode always has 50% of the cases below it. (S)

_____ 8. In a distribution with a negative skew, the tail is to the left. (N)

_____ 9. Since income is skewed in large populations, the median rather than the mean is usually used for describing average income. (C)

_____ 10. The mode is the type of average most likely to be reported in a scientific article. (A)

_____ 11. It is possible for a given distribution to have more than one mode. (H)

_____ 12. In a distribution with a negative skew, the mode has a higher value than the median. (F)

_____ 13. In a distribution with a positive skew, the tail is to the right. (R)

_____ 14. The mode is the least reliable average. (Y)

Write the answer to the riddle here, putting one letter on each line:

TO BECOME A _____ _____ _____ _____ _____ _____   _____ _____ _____

NOTES:

Dr. P.'s friendly advice: ARE YOU ALL EARS IN STATISTICS?

Practice being an ACTIVE listener. Think about what is being said and try to relate it to something you already know or understand. For example, when your instructor first mentions the "standard deviation" think about the everyday meaning of each word in the term. A "standard" is something you measure with. A "deviation" is a difference from some norm.

As easy as this piece of advice seems, some people have trouble implementing it. The next time you use it, record an example here:

_____

_____

Share this with your study group. You will learn from each other how to use this important learning tool.

Name: _____ Date: _____

Worksheet 13: RANGE, STANDARD DEVIATION (S), AND VARIANCE

RIDDLE: What did the control tower say to the jet that was on fire?

Directions: To find the answer to the riddle, write the answers to the problems on the lines. The word in the solution section beside the answer to the first problem is the first word in the answer to the riddle, the word beside the answer to the second problem is the second word, and so on.

 Use "high minus low plus one" to compute the range. Each group is an entire population. Round the standard deviations to two decimal places. Square the standard deviations in order to obtain the variances. Round the variances to one decimal place.

Population E's scores: 0, 11, 7, 7, 8, 11, 5, 10
Population F's scores: 2, 2, 25, 9, 25, 9, 15, 5, 20
Population G's scores: 8, 9, 9, 10, 12, 10, 12, 12, 12, 11

1. What is the range of Population E's scores? _____

2. What is the standard deviation of Population E's scores? _____

3. What is the variance of Population E's scores? _____

4. What is the range of Population F's scores? _____

5. What is the standard deviation of Population F's scores? _____

6. What is the variance of Population F's scores? _____

7. What is the range of Population G's scores? _____

8. What is the standard deviation of Population G' s scores? _____

9. What is the variance of Population G's scores? _____

SOLUTION SECTION:

12 (REPEAT)   10 (LAS VEGAS)   27.404 (WE)   3.42 (AFTER)   5 (ART)

24 (OUR)   9.39 (BROKE)   11.7 (ME)   1.8 (POKER)   19 (SORRY)

2.9 (SAD)   4 (FRIENDLY)   1.43 (IN)   2.0 (HEAVEN)   78.01 (IS)

7.2 (GUM)   75.0 (WHO)   8.66 (FATHER)   675.55 (CARDS)   14.32 (BE)

Write the answer to the riddle here, putting one word on each line:

_____ _____ _____: "_____ _____ _____ _____ _____ _____...."

NOTES:

Dr. P.'s friendly advice: LOOK BEFORE YOU LEAP!

Before you begin to do computations, examine the raw data carefully. Be sure you understand what they represent. For example, if you are asked for the standard deviation, it is important to know whether the scores represent an entire population or just a sample; you need to know this in order to select the right formula.

Also, estimate the probable outcome of your computations. Are the differences among the scores small? Then you will expect a low value for the standard deviation. Use this as a partial check on your answer.

Practice estimating the answer the next time you compute the standard deviation and write the outcome here:

Worksheet number, problem number: _____ , _____

Your estimate: relatively large or small? _____

Actual outcome: _____

Name: _____ Date: _____

Worksheet 14: UNBIASED ESTIMATE OF STANDARD DEVIATION (s)

RIDDLE: Why were the Dark Ages so very dark?

Directions: To find the answer to the riddle, write the answers to the problems on the lines. The word in the solution section beside the answer to the first problem is the first word in the answer to the riddle, the word beside the answer to the second problem is the second word, and so on.
    Each of the following is a sample from a population. Calculate the unbiased estimate of each population's standard deviation. Round your answers to two decimal places.

```
Sample H: 1, 4, 5, 2, 9
Sample I: 3, 6, 0, 9, 10, 1
Sample J: 5, 6, 7, 8, 6, 7, 8
Sample K: 20, 15, 25, 20, 15, 25
Sample L: 20, 0, 30, 20, 15, 30
Sample M: 30, 30, 30, 30
```

1. For H, what is the standard deviation? _____

2. For I, what is the standard deviation? _____

3. For J, what is the standard deviation? _____

4. For K, what is the standard deviation? _____

5. For L, what is the standard deviation? _____

6. For M, what is the standard deviation? _____

SOLUTION SECTION:

9.70 (MOON)   17.37 (LIGHT)   11.14 (MANY)   4.47 (SO)

1.24 (SUN)   4.17 (THERE)   20.00 (HAPPENED)   1.11 (WERE)

124.17 (DAMSELS)   0.00 (KNIGHTS)   3.25 (ELECTRICITY)

3.11 (BECAUSE)   10.00 (BULBS)   52.00 (CLOUDS)

Write the answer to the riddle here, putting one word on each line:

_____ _____ _____ _____ _____ _____

NOTES:

Dr. P.'s friendly advice: SO YOU'RE SICK AND DECIDE TO STAY HOME BY THE FIRE.

As soon as you're feeling better, call at least two classmates to find out what you missed. Just one won't do; the human race is notorious for its forgetfulness.

Then read your text and do as much of the assigned work as you can. Read the entire section covering the lecture you missed even if you can't understand everything. By reading all the way through the section, you will at least get an overview, and this will help prevent that "lost feeling" when you return to class.

Finally, call your professor if you have some questions that can be handled over the phone. Visit your professor during office hours.

RECORD THE INFORMATION YOU WILL NEED IF YOU ARE OUT ILL:

Names and phone numbers of students you plan to contact:

_____

_____

Telephone number and office number of your professor:

_____

Name: _____ Date: _____

Worksheet 15: STANDARD DEVIATION: CONCEPTS

RIDDLE: What's the main problem with the "rat race?"

Directions: To find the answer to the riddle, write "T" for "true" or "F" for "false" on the line to the left of each statement. The word at the end of the first true statement is the first word in the answer to the riddle, the word at the end of the second true statement is the second word, and so on.

_____ 1. The standard deviation is more descriptive of a normal distribution than it is descriptive of a skewed distribution. (EVEN)

_____ 2. A normal distribution is symmetrical. (IF)

_____ 3. The square root of the standard deviation is called the variance. (BUSINESS)

_____ 4. In a normal distribution, about 68% of the cases lie between the mean and one standard deviation unit above the mean. (TRAP)

_____ 5. In a normal distribution, about 95% of the cases lie between one standard deviation above the mean and one standard deviation below the mean. (WEALTH)

_____ 6. If two groups are being compared, the group with the larger standard deviation has more variability. (YOU)

_____ 7. If M = 50.0 and S = 10.0, about 34% of the cases in a normal distribution lie between scores of 40 and 50. (WIN)

_____ 8. If M = 32.0 and S = 5.0, about 34% of the cases in a normal distribution lie between scores of 27 and 32. (YOU'RE)

_____ 9. If M = 100.0 and S = 15.0, about 68% of the cases in a normal distribution lie between 66 and 134. (QUICKLY)

_____ 10. If M = 500.0 and S = 100.0, about 68% of the cases in a normal distribution lie between 400 and 600. (STILL)

_____ 11. The standard deviation was designed to describe skewed distributions. (LOST)

_____ 12. Three standard deviation units on both sides of the mean includes over 99% of the area in a normal distribution. (A)

_____ 13. The standard deviation is usually associated with the mean. That is, if the mean is used to describe the average, the standard deviation is usually used to describe the variability. (RAT)

Write the answer to the riddle here, putting one word on each line:

_____ _____ _____ _____ , _____ _____

_____ _____

TAKE NOTE OF THIS!

Dr. P.'s friendly advice: TIPS FOR TAKING CLASS NOTES.

If you're busy trying to write down every word your professor says, you probably won't have time to be an active listener, thinking about what is being said and how it relates to what you already know.

Here are two important things you can do to become a more efficient note taker:

1. Read all assigned readings in advance of a lecture. Then you will know what is covered in the textbook, which usually does not need to be written in your notes. You will recognize when your professor is providing additional information and examples which you may need to include in your notes.

2. Master statistical symbols as soon as you encounter them. Use them when taking notes. It is much more efficient to record a symbol in your notes than the word or words for which it stands.

Try this example. Suppose your instructor says, "In order to compute the semi-interquartile range or quartile deviation, you must first compute the 25th and 75th centiles." Rewrite the statement, substituting symbols for the three statistics named. Also, omit any words that are not essential for comprehension of the statement:

_____

_____

Name: _____   Date: _____

Worksheet 16: QUARTILE DEVIATION (SEMI-INTERQUARTILE RANGE)

RIDDLE: What does the moon do in order to make people think he is clever?

Directions: To find the answer to the riddle, write the answers to the problems on the lines. The word in the solution section beside the answer to the first problem is the first word in the answer to the riddle, the word beside the answer to the second problem is the second word, and so on.

Round centiles to three decimal places. Round quartile deviations to two decimal places.

Group A		Group B		Group C	
X	f	X	f	X	f
13	1	30	16	36–38	2
12	0	29	8	33–35	1
11	3	28	4	30–32	2
10	6	27	0	27–29	3
9	8	26	3	24–26	0
8	9	25	1	21–23	4
7	21	24	2	18–20	7
6	32			15–17	8
5	40			12–14	10
				9–11	11
				6–8	15
				3–5	20

1. What is the value of the 25th centile for Group A? _____

2. What is the value of the 75th centile for Group A? _____

CONTINUED

3. What is the value of the quartile deviation for Group A? _____

4. What is the value of the 25th centile for Group B? _____

5. What is the value of the 75th centile for Group B? _____

6. What is the value of the quartile deviation for Group B? _____

7. What is the value of the 25th centile for Group C? _____

8. What is the value of the 75th centile for Group C? _____

9. What is the value of the quartile deviation for Group C? _____

SOLUTION SECTION:

7.357 (IS)   5.60 (SIDE)   4.82 (AM)   6.15 (FEELING)   5.650 (HIS)

5.250 (HE)   0.92 (ONLY)   29.969 (SHOW)   14.344 (NIGHT)   1.84 (SUN)

11.19 (FOOL)   1.05 (CAREFUL)   28.125 (TO)   15.281 (BE)   9.357 (GLOW)

28.969 (FACE)   27.625 (MAN)   16.844 (BRIGHT)   32.123 (IN)   9.19 (FOR)

Write the answer to the riddle here, putting one word on each line:

_____   _____   _____   _____   _____   _____

_____   _____   _____

Name: _____   Date: _____

Worksheet 17: STANDARD SCORES

RIDDLE: What's the problem with joining the paratroopers?

Directions: To find the answer to the riddle, write the answers to the problems on the lines. The word in the solution section beside the answer to the first problem is the first word in the answer to the riddle, the word beside the answer to the second problem is the second word, and so on. Round your answers to one decimal place.

RAW SCORE STATISTICS:
        Group A: M = 20.00, S = 2.00   Group C: M = 50.00, S = 6.00
        Group B: M = 33.33, S = 3.41   Group D: M = 62.85, S = 6.52

_____ 1. What is the z-score of a person with a raw score of 20 in Group A?

_____ 2. What is the z-score of a person with a raw score of 24 in Group A?

_____ 3. What is the z-score of a person with a raw score of 22 in Group B?

_____ 4. What is the z-score of a person with a raw score of 53 in Group C?

_____ 5. What is the z-score of a person with a raw score of 70 in Group D?

RAW SCORE STATISTICS (One group took both tests.):
        Reading Test: M = 30.00, S = 3.00
        Math Test: M = 40.00, S = 4.00

_____ 6. Jan has raw scores of 33 on reading and 34 on math. She is higher on reading than math by how many standard score points?

_____ 7. John has raw scores of 30 on reading and 44 on math. He is higher on math than reading by how many standard score points?

_____ 8. Kelly has raw scores of 36 on reading and 36 on math. She is higher on reading than math by how many standard score points?

_____ 9. Rich has raw scores of 25 on reading and 42 on math. He is higher on math than reading by how many standard score points?

SOLUTION SECTION:

2.0 (HAVE)   3.3 (FLY)   −0.5 (PLANE)   0.0 (YOU)   1.7 (FORCE)   0.5 (DO)

1.1 (EVERYTHING)   −1.1 (PARACHUTE)   −2.0 (JUMP)   −3.3 (TO)   2.2 (TIME)

2.5 (RIGHT)   1.0 (THE)   −1.5 (DEFENSE)   3.0 (FIRST)   4.0 (GLIDE)

Write the answer to the riddle here, putting one word on each line:

_____ _____ _____ _____ _____ _____

_____ _____ _____

NOTES:

Dr. P.'s friendly advice: HOW CAN YOU AVOID THE BEACHED-WHALE FEELING?

Proper study and work habits are the keys. You'll find solid advice on these practices throughout this workbook. It's up to you to implement the advice.

Take a few moments right now to review all the advice you've read on the preceding pages. Identify the most appropriate category shown below for each piece of advice. Record the number of the worksheet facing each study skill essay.

1. Advice fully implemented: _____

2. Advice partially implemented: _____

3. Advice not implemented: _____

Identify one piece of advice from categories 2 or 3 that you will begin implementing today. Record its number here: _____

Name: _____ Date: _____

Worksheet 18: TRANSFORMED STANDARD SCORES

RIDDLE: What do you get if you cross a jeweler and plumber?

Directions: To find the answer to the riddle, write the answers to the problems on the lines. The letter in the solution section beside the answer to the first problem is the first letter in the answer to the riddle, the letter beside the answer to the second problem is the second letter, and so on.
    Round your answers to one decimal place.

RAW SCORE STATISTICS:

    Sample Y: M = 22.00, s = 2.00   Sample L: M = 28.00, s = 4.00

    Sample K: M = 25.00, s = 1.50   Sample P: M = 30.00, s = 6.00

_____ 1. A person in Sample Y with a raw score of 24 has what transformed standard score on a new scale with M = 100 and s = 15?

_____ 2. A person in Sample Y with a raw score of 18 has what transformed standard score on a new scale with M = 100 and s = 15?

_____ 3. A person in Sample K with a raw score of 24 has what transformed standard score on a new scale with M = 100 and s = 15?

_____ 4. A person in Sample L with a raw score of 24 has what transformed standard score on a new scale with M = 100 and s = 15?

_____ 5. A person in Sample P with a raw score of 30 has what transformed standard score on a new scale with M = 100 and s = 15?

_____ 6. A person in Sample Y with a raw score of 27 has what transformed standard score on a new scale with M = 50 and s = 10?

_____ 7. A person in Sample K with a raw score of 27 has what transformed standard score on a new scale with M = 50 and s = 10?

_____ 8. A person in Sample L with a raw score of 27 has what transformed standard score on a new scale with M = 50 and s = 10?

_____ 9. A person in Sample P with a raw score of 36 has what transformed standard score on a new scale with M = 500 and s = 100?

CONTINUED

Worksheet 18: Continued

_____ 10. A person in Sample K with a raw score of 25 has what transformed
standard score on a new scale with M = 500 and s = 100?

_____ 11. A person in Sample L with a raw score of 22 has what transformed
standard score on a new scale with M = 500 and s = 100?

SOLUTION SECTION:

350.0 (G)	600.0 (I)	130.0 (Y)	47.5 (R)	110.0 (P)
500.0 (N)	25.0 (M)	63.3 (B)	52.5 (X)	650.0 (Z)
115.0 (B)	70.0 (A)	400.0 (K)	90.0 (T)	100.0 (T)
85.0 (H)	551.0 (F)	50.0 (G)	75.0 (U)	900.0 (J)

Write the answer to the riddle here, putting one letter on each line:

____ ____ ____ ____   ____ ____ ____   ____ ____ ____ ____

Name: _____   Date: _____

Worksheet 19: AREAS UNDER THE NORMAL CURVE: I

RIDDLE: There are two rules in life about buses. The first is: "If you're waiting for a
         bus, it never comes." What's the second one?

Directions: To find the answer to the riddle, write the answers to the problems on the
lines. The word in the solution section beside the answer to the first problem is the first
word in the answer to the riddle, the word beside the answer to the second problem is the
second word, and so on.
     For each standard score (z-score) given below, write the proportion that lies in the
area under the normal curve between the standard score and the mean.

    1. z = 1.96 _____   7. z = -2.50 _____

    2. z = 3.00 _____   8. z = 0.00 _____

    3. z = 2.58 _____   9. z = -0.44 _____

    4. z = 1.00 _____   10. z = -1.50 _____

    5. z = -0.50 _____   11. z = 1.75 _____

    6. z = -0.60 _____   12. z = 1.60 _____

SOLUTION SECTION:

0.4970 (AS)   0.4066 (MULE)   0.2734 (A)   0.4875 (BY)

0.4998 (WAITING)   0.4965 (KICKED)   0.4938 (ALWAYS)

0.4452 (YOU)   0.4599 (OF)   0.1700 (IN)   0.4332 (FRONT)

0.4750 (WHEN)   0.2257 (IS)   0.1915 (BUS)   0.4987 (YOU'RE)

0.3413 (THE)   0.4951 (DRIVING)   0.0000 (RIGHT)

Write the answer to the riddle here, putting one word on each line:

_____ _____ _____, _____ _____ _____

_____ _____ _____ _____ _____ _____

NOTES:

Dr. P.'s friendly advice: USING A COMPUTER IN STATISTICS?

Here's a self-test for you. Check those that apply.

_____ 1. Do you review the data before entering it in order to make mental estimates of the outcomes you expect? (This will be most helpful when you are analyzing only a small number of scores.)

_____ 2. Do you always review and edit the data you've entered before you instruct the computer to perform the calculations? (Entering a single incorrect score will result in a wrong answer.)

_____ 3. Do you always review the documentation for using a program before beginning to use it? (Even friendly programs sometimes have a catch or two.)

_____ 4. Are you always careful to follow each and every step in the order indicated in the documentation? (If the documentation belongs to you, check off each step as you do it.)

_____ 5. Do you avoid the temptation to blame the computer or program for incorrect answers? (Most mistakes are due to errors made by the users, who need to check their data and procedures.)

What's your total score? (One point for each check.): _____

Name: _____   Date: _____

Worksheet 20: AREAS UNDER THE NORMAL CURVE: II

RIDDLE: What do tongues have to do with friendship?

Directions: To find the answer to the riddle, write the answers to the problems on the lines. The word in the solution section beside the answer to the first problem is the first word in the answer to the riddle, the word beside the answer to the second problem is the second word, and so on.

    For each pair of standard scores (z-scores) given below, write the proportion that lies between them under the normal curve.

1. 1.00 and -1.00? _____   8. 1.00 and 0.50? _____

2. 1.96 and -1.96? _____   9. -1.00 and -2.00? _____

3. 2.58 and -2.58? _____   10 0.75 and 0.50? _____

4. 0.00 and 1.00? _____   11. -2.00 and -3.00? _____

5. 2.00 and -2.00? _____   12. -1.60 and -2.60? _____

6. 3.00 and -3.00? _____   13. 2.50 and 1.96? _____

7. 0.00 and 3.00? _____

SOLUTION SECTION:

0.0188 (FRIENDS)   0.0501 (THEIR)   0.4750 (RELATIONSHIPS)

0.9759 (AM)   0.0215 (KEEPING)   0.0819 (TROUBLE)   0.1359 (ANY)

0.5328 (HIS)   0.8185 (US)   0.1498 (HAVE)   0.9974 (TONGUES)

0.4987 (SELDOM)   0.9500 (WHO)   0.4649 (YES)   0.9902 (CAN)

0.6826 (PEOPLE)   0.3413 (HOLD)   0.9688 (SPEAK)   0.9544 (THEIR)

Write the answer to the riddle here, putting one word on each line:

_____ _____ _____ _____ _____ _____ _____

_____ _____ _____ _____ _____ _____

Dr P.'s friendly advice: STATISTICS GOT YOU STRESSED OUT?

All normal people feel at least a little stress when studying a technical and important subject like statistics.

If you think that you are feeling more than your share and that the stress is debilitating, follow these steps:

1. Close your eyes and feel yourself breathe. Concentrate on your breathing for at least 30 seconds.

2. Try to visualize in your mind a pleasant place. If you can't see it in your mind's eye, think about what it is you like about the place.

3. Finally, silently repeat several times, "When I open my eyes I will feel relaxed," or some other thought that is comforting to you.

Right after you try this, make an anecdotal record by filling in the blanks:

Date: _____   Beginning and ending times: _____ _____

Place: _____   Was the place quiet? _____

Could you clearly feel yourself breathing? _____

What did you try to visualize? _____

What did you repeat to yourself? _____

Did you feel less anxious at the end? _____

Make a record like the above for the first five times you try this technique. For some people, it takes practice to get the full benefit.

TRY IT. YOU'LL LIKE IT!

Name: _____ Date: _____

Worksheet 21: AREAS UNDER THE NORMAL CURVE: III

RIDDLE: What causes most auto accidents?

Directions: To find the answer to the riddle, write the answers to the problems on the lines. The word in the solution section beside the answer to the first problem is the first word in the answer to the riddle, the word beside the answer to the second problem is the second word, and so on.

Each question refers to the percent of cases under the normal curve.

_____ 1. % above a z of 1.00?   _____ 5. % below a z of 0.00?

_____ 2. % below a z of 2.00?   _____ 6. % above a z of 1.96?

_____ 3. % below a z of 0.50?   _____ 7. % below a z of -2.58?

_____ 4. % below a z of -0.60?   _____ 8. % above a z of -1.75?

_____ 9. If a person has a raw score of 53 and if the raw score M = 49.00 and S = 4.00, what percent is below the person's z-score?

_____ 10. If a person has a raw score of 89 and if the raw score M = 99.00 and S = 5.00, what percent is below the person's z-score?

_____ 11. If a person has a raw score of 450 and if the raw score M =500.00 and S = 100.00, what percent is below the person's z score?

SOLUTION SECTION:

15.87% (PEOPLE)   100.00% (WALKING)   97.72% (WHO)   27.43% (IN)

97.50% (SEE)   4.90% (ROADS)   69.15% (DRIVE)   0.49% (THEIR)

50.00% (HIGH)   45.99% (ROUGH)   2.50% (WHILE)   2.28% (IN)

84.13% (ARE)   30.85% (NEUTRAL)   95.99% (MINDS)   34.13% (HER)

Write the answer to the riddle here, putting one word on each line:

_____ _____ _____ _____ _____ _____

_____ _____ _____ _____ _____

NOTES:

Dr. P.'s friendly advice: FEELING OVERWHELMED BY STATISTICS?

Here's a suggestion that should help: For each study session (whether it's independent, with a tutor, or with your study group) set a reasonable goal--something that can be accomplished in about 45 minutes or less.

EXAMPLES: 1. Understand percentile ranks and compute them.
2. Learn how to compute the median without referring to the textbook example.

Work until you have met your goal.
Having a goal that you have reached will give you a sense of accomplishment. It will help you focus on what you do know--instead of what you don't know--about statistics. Try it; you'll feel less overwhelmed.

Make your plans here for your next independent study session:

Where will you study? _____ Date: _____

Beginning time: _____ Approximate ending time: _____

Your goal: _____

Name: _____ Date: _____

Worksheet 22: PERCENTILE RANKS

RIDDLE: Why is "dough" the wrong term for money?

Directions: To find the answer to the riddle, write the answers to the problems on the lines. The word in the solution section beside the answer to the first problem is the first word in the answer to the riddle, the word beside the answer to the second problem is the second word, and so on.

    Calculate the exact percentile ranks; do not estimate them from a cumulative percentage curve. Round your answers to one decimal place.

X	f
45-47	2
42-44	1
39-41	3
36-38	14
33-35	15
30-32	12
27-29	9
24-26	7
21-23	4

_____ 1. What is the percentile rank of a person with a score of 31?

_____ 2. What is the percentile rank of a person with a score of 42?

_____ 3. What is the percentile rank of a person with a score of 26?

_____ 4. What is the percentile rank of a person with a score of 41?

_____ 5. What is the percentile rank of a person with a score of 23?

SOLUTION SECTION:

56.7 (BAKE)	35.8 (RICH)	9.3 (DOLLARS)	25.07 (SAVINGS)
38.8 (DOUGH)	5.0 (HANDS)	13.0 (FEET)	23.4 (WEALTH)
95.8 (STICKS)	61.1 (IS)	94.8 (YOUR)	14.6 (TO)
20.1 (LIFELESS)	4.0 (RICHES)	2.0 (BAKERY)	1.0 (HELP)

Write the answer to the riddle here, putting one word on each line:

Because _____ _____ _____ _____ _____

NOTES:

	Test A	Test B
Jane	50	40
Slim	45	38
Jake	42	35
Saul	42	30
Lucy	38	20
Mica	34	19
Mike	31	19

Dr. P.'s friendly advice: DON'T FORGET TO MAKE MENTAL ESTIMATES OF ANSWERS.

When you have only a small amount of data, you often can make good estimates and use them as partial checks on your work with a computer or calculator.

For the data shown above, make mental estimates (no calculators, please) and answer these questions:

1. Suppose you calculated the mean on Test A to be 32.32. Would this be a good answer? _____

2. Suppose you calculated the Pearson r and obtained an r of -0.90. Would this be a good answer? _____

3. Suppose you calculated the Pearson r and obtained an r of 0.11. Would this be a good answer? _____

If you're not sure how to make mental estimates in order to answer the three questions shown above, discuss this page with your study group or other classmates.

Name: _____ Date: _____

Worksheet 23: PEARSON r: COMPUTATIONS

RIDDLE: At the dining room table, the mother said, "Stop reaching. Haven't you got a
tongue?" What did the son say in return?

Directions: To find the answer to the riddle, write the answers to the problems on the lines.
The word in the solution section beside the answer to the first problem is the first word in
the answer to the riddle, the word beside the answer to the second problem is the second
word, and so on.
    Round your answers to two decimal places.

X	Y		A	B
3	6		20	0
5	8		15	0
4	9		10	5
9	10		18	2
10	12		9	10
			6	15

C	D		E	F
6	1		35	8
1	0		41	8
10	20		55	9
15	25		50	10
20	25		35	10
25	25		30	10

CONTINUED

G	H		I	J
10	3		11	0
9	1		14	0
8	3		7	0
7	4		2	0
6	7		1	0
5	7		15	0
0	7			

_____ 1. What is the value of the Pearson r for X and Y?

_____ 2. What is the value of the Pearson r for A and B?

_____ 3. What is the value of the Pearson r for C and D?

_____ 4. What is the value of the Pearson r for E and F?

_____ 5. What is the value of the Pearson r for G and H?

_____ 6. What is the value of the Pearson r for I and J?

SOLUTION SECTION:

1.00 (PLEASE)	0.78 (PASS)	-0.87 (FATHER)	0.00 (LONGER)
-0.78 (ARE)	-0.24 (LEGS)	-0.90 (BUT)	0.87 (MY)
0.10 (MANNERS)	-0.04 (ARMS)	-0.95 (IS)	-.25 (FOOD)
0.90 (YES)	-1.00 (TABLE)	-0.11 (FEET)	0.50 (DINNER)

Write the answer to the riddle here, putting one word on each line:

_____ , _____ _____ _____ _____ _____

Name: _____ Date: _____

Worksheet 24: PEARSON r: INTERPRETATION: I

RIDDLE: What kind of cow gives evaporated milk?

Directions: To find the answer to the riddle, write "T" for "true" or "F" for "false" on the line to the left of each statement. The letter at the end of the first true statement is the first letter in the answer to the riddle, the letter at the end of the second true statement is the second letter, and so on.

_____ 1. A Pearson r of 1.00 represents no relationship. (M)

_____ 2. A Pearson r of 0.50, is more likely to be called "moderately strong" than to be called "weak." (A)

_____ 3. A Pearson r of -0.50 is more likely to be called "moderately strong" than to be called "weak." (D)

_____ 4. A Pearson r of -0.97 represents a very weak relationship. (E)

_____ 5. A Pearson r indicates both the strength and direction of a relationship. (R)

_____ 6. A Pearson r is a type of correlation coefficient. (Y)

_____ 7. If a relationship is extremely strong, a Pearson r will have a value greater than 1.00. (I)

_____ 8. A Pearson r of 0.95 represents a very strong relationship. (C)

_____ 9. The maximum value of a Pearson r is 0.00. (F)

_____ 10. The possible values of a Pearson r range from -1.00 to 1.00. (O)

_____ 11. The purpose of a Pearson r is to establish the central tendency of a set of scores. (P)

_____ 12. All negative relationships are weak. (D)

_____ 13. A scatter diagram with dots that form a pattern going from the lower left-hand corner to the upper right-hand corner represents scores that would yield a positive value of r. (W)

_____ 14. If a Pearson r between two variables is very strong, this provides very firm evidence that one variable affects the other. (S)

Write the answer to the riddle here, putting one letter on each line:

_____   _____ _____ _____   _____ _____ _____

NOTES:

IT'S GOING TO BE A GREAT WEEKEND!

Dr. P.'s friendly advice: EVERYONE DESERVES A BREAK!

But if you could set aside just 20 minutes (more if possible) each on a busy Saturday and Sunday for a little work on statistics, you might learn more than you expected--and you might have an even better weekend, knowing that you're making progress in statistics.

Set a goal for each of the two study sessions. For example, each of these is an appropriate goal for a short study session: (1) "Be able to interpret Pearson r's" and (2) "Build speed in computing standard scores."

By setting reasonable goals, weekend study sessions won't seem like major chores.

RECORD HERE YOUR STUDY PLANS FOR THIS WEEKEND:

Saturday: Time for study: _____ Place: _____

Goal: _____

Sunday: Time for study: _____ Place: _____

Goal: _____

Name: _____ Date: _____

Worksheet 25: PEARSON r: INTERPRETATION: II

RIDDLE: Why did the hippies get married in a bath tub?

Directions: To find the answer to the riddle, write "T" for "true" or "F" for "false" on the line to the left of each statement. The word at the end of the first true statement is the first word in the answer to the riddle, the word at the end of the second true statement is the second word, and so on.

_____ 1. For a Pearson r of 0.50, the coefficient of determination equals 0.25. (IN)

_____ 2. For a Pearson r of -0.60, the coefficient of determination equals 0.36. (ORDER)

_____ 3. For a Pearson r of 0.75, 75% of the variance on one variable is explained by (i.e., is accounted for by) the other. (LOVE)

_____ 4. For a Pearson r of -0.40, 40% of the variance on one variable is explained by the other. (WILL)

_____ 5. For a Pearson r of 0.90, 81% of the variance on one variable is explained by the other. (TO)

_____ 6. For a Pearson r of 0.80, 36% of the variance on one variable is NOT explained by the other. (HAVE)

_____ 7. The Pearson r may be thought of as a proportion that, when multiplied by 100, yields the percent of variance on one variable explained by the other. (BECOME)

_____ 8. The square of the Pearson r is known as the "coefficient of determination." (A)

_____ 9. For a Pearson r of -0.36, the coefficient of determination equals -0.06. (COUPLE)

_____ 10. For a Pearson r of -0.22, about 95% of the variance on one variable is NOT explained by the other. (DOUBLE)

_____ 11. For a Pearson r of -0.62, a majority of the variance on one variable is explained by the other. (CLEAN)

_____ 12. For making predictions from one variable to another, a Pearson r of -0.78 is better than a Pearson r of 0.52. (RING)

_____ 13. A simple correlational study is usually NOT suitable for identifying cause-and-effect relationships. (CEREMONY)

Write the answer to the riddle here, putting one word on each line:

_____ _____ _____ _____ _____ _____

_____ _____

NOTES:

Dr. P.'s friendly advice: ARE SOME OF YOUR ANSWERS AS IMPROBABLE AS THIS MAN'S COSTUME?

Some statistics have limits. If you obtain answers outside of them you'll know immediately that your answer is wrong. This awareness is especially helpful when taking tests.

Check your knowledge of limits. Check off each of the following answers that is improbable.

_____ 1. r = 1.44	_____ 4. s = 5.67
_____ 2. r = -0.65	_____ 5. z-score = 54.98
_____ 3. s = -3.14	_____ 6. z-score = 1.44

Did you check all the odd-numbered items? Remember a Pearson r cannot exceed a value of one; a standard deviation cannot be negative; z-scores above three are rare.

Name: _____ Date: _____

Worksheet 26: SPEARMAN'S RANK-ORDER CORRELATION

RIDDLE: What's the wacky definition of a "honeymoon?"

Directions: To find the answer to the riddle, write the answers to the problems on the lines. The word in the solution section beside the answer to the first problem is the first word in the answer to the riddle, the word beside the answer to the second problem is the second word, and so on.

Rank scores from high to low.

Scores: 20, 20, 25, 29, 30, 35, 35, 35, 39, 40, 40

_____ 1. What is the rank for a score of 20?
_____ 2. What is the rank for a score of 30?
_____ 3. What is the rank for a score of 35?
_____ 4. What is the rank for a score of 39?
_____ 5. What is the rank for a score of 40?

	Rank on A	Rank on B	Score on C
Ruby	1	2	60
Saul	2	1	58
Frank	3	3	35
Sally	4	5	35
Millie	5	6	15
Rafe	6	4	22

_____ 6. What's the value of the rank-order correlation between A and B?
_____ 7. What's the value of the rank-order correlation between A and C?
_____ 8. What's the value of the rank-order correlation between B and C?

SOLUTION SECTION:

6 (LOVE)   4.5 (BEING)   9.5 (WEDDING)   10.5 (A)   7 (PERIOD)

-0.77 (TUNNEL)   0.84 (DEBATING)   0.77 (DATING)   5 (OF)

1.5 (BETWEEN)   1 (ARE)   0.93 (AND)   -0.22 (TREES)

3 (DOTING)   1.5 (BETWEEN)   0.60 (WELL)   0.38 (FAMILY)

Write the answer to the riddle here, putting one word on each line:

_____ _____ _____ _____ _____ _____

_____ _____

NOTES:

Dr. P.'s friendly advice: AVOID THIS FEELING AT EXAM TIME!

Here's how:

1. Find out as much as your instructor is willing to share about the exam as soon as it is announced.

2. Try to anticipate what is likely to be asked and prepare for these questions. Concepts and computations that were stressed in class are likely to be tested.

3. Study regularly. Set aside a specific time each day for study. Mark the times on your calendar and keep your appointments for study just as faithfully as you would keep your appointments with a dentist!

Circle the choice that indicates how well prepared you are right now for your next exam in statistics:

Very well prepared   5   4   3   2   1   Not at all prepared

Following the advice on study skills in this book will increase your preparedness rating.

Name: _____ Date: _____

Worksheet 27: MULTIPLE LINEAR CORRELATION: TWO PREDICTORS

RIDDLE: How do you know when a restaurant is clean?

Directions: To find the answer to the riddle, write the answers to the problems on the lines. The word in the solution section beside the answer to the first problem is the first word in the answer to the riddle, the word beside the answer to the second problem is the second word, and so on.
  The tables show Pearson r's. Round your answers to two decimal places.

	1	2	3		4	5	6		7	8	9
1		.440	.250	4		.500	.600	7		.340	.290
2			.100	5			.200	8			.500

	10	11	12		13	14	15		16	17	18
10		.271	.245	13		.171	.204	16		.918	.957
11			.164	14			.160	17			.823

_____ 1. What is the value of R for predicting Variable 1 using the best-weighted combination of Variables 2 and 3?

_____ 2. What is the value of R for predicting Variable 4 using the best-weighted combination of Variables 5 and 6?

_____ 3. What is the value of R for predicting Variable 7 using the best-weighted combination of Variables 8 and 9?

_____ 4. What is the value of R for predicting Variable 10 using the best-weighted combination of Variables 11 and 12?

_____ 5. What is the value of R for predicting Variable 13 using the best-weighted combination of Variables 14 and 15?

_____ 6. What is the value of R for predicting Variable 16 using the best-weighted combination of Variables 17 and 18?

SOLUTION SECTION:

1.00 (EAT)   0.11 (WASH)   0.18 (HUNGRY)   0.49 (WHEN)

0.37 (FOOD)   0.54 (RESTAURANT)   0.34 (TASTES)   0.85 (IS)

0.71 (THE)   0.59 (WAITRESS)   0.25 (LIKE)   0.79 (AM)

0.65 (MENU)   0.98 (SOAP)   0.62 (PORTION)   0.88 (SICK)

Write the answer to the riddle here, putting one word on each line:

_____ _____ _____ _____ _____ _____

NOTES:

Dr. P.'s friendly advice: SIZE ALSO MAKES A BIG DIFFERENCE IN STATISTICS!

Pay careful attention to whether letters used to identify statistics are upper-case or lower-case. Lower-case "f" stands for "frequency;" upper-case "F" stands for an important statistic you'll learn about later in the course.

Be careful to notice the case when you read and use formulas.

Here are a few you may have already learned about. Write what each one means:

X: _____   x: _____

R: _____   r: _____

S: _____   s: _____

Name: _____   Date: _____

Worksheet 28: LINEAR REGRESSION

RIDDLE: How did the tree surgeon hurt his back?

Directions: To find the answer to the riddle, write the answers to the problems on the lines. The word in the solution section beside the answer to the first problem is the first word in the answer to the riddle, the word beside the answer to the second problem is the second word, and so on.

Round the answers for slopes and intercepts to two decimal places. Round predicted scores to one decimal place.

	X	Y		TEST	GPA
Gert	20	9	Saul	20	3.00
George	10	3	Sam	15	2.00
Grant	5	0	Sally	10	1.00
			Sue	11	0.00

_____ 1. What is the value of the slope for predicting Y from X?

_____ 2. What is the value of the intercept for predicting Y from X?

_____ 3. What is the predicted score on Y for a person with a score on X of 7?

_____ 4. What is the predicted score on Y for a person with a score on X of 17?

_____ 5. What is the value of the slope for predicting GPA from the test?

_____ 6. What is the value of the intercept for predicting GPA from the test?

_____ 7. What is the predicted GPA for a person with a score of 12 on the test?

_____ 8. What is the predicted GPA for a person with a score of 18 on the test?

_____ 9. What is the predicted GPA for a person with a score of 14 on the test?

SOLUTION SECTION:

-20.4 (MEDICAL)   -1.11 (FLY)   1.5 (PATIENT)   0.60 (WHILE)

3.00 (NURSE)   2.11 (BRANCHES)   1.2 (SURGERY)   7.2 (HE)

-1.5 (OPERATION)   -3.00 (PERFORMING)   0.26 (FELL)   1.0 (OF)

2.6 (HIS)   -2.11 (OUT)   -2.6 (SCREAM)   5.66 (LEAVES)

Write the answer to the riddle here, putting one word on each line:

_____ _____ _____ _____ _____ _____

_____ _____ _____

NOTES:

Dr. P.'s friendly advice: DOES STATISTICS SEEM LIKE A MAZE TO YOU?

It could be that you are not paying enough attention to the vocabulary of statistics.

Like any specialized field, statistics has many technical terms. After they've been introduced to you, your instructor and textbook author will use many of them over and over in various contexts throughout the semester. You'll get lost if you don't master new terms as soon as you encounter them.

Name a term you heard for the first time in the last lecture:

_____

Define the term from memory:

_____

Look up the term in your notes and textbook. Write a corrected definition here:

_____

You can simulate these steps by making study cards with terms on the front and correct definitions on the back.

Name: _____ Date: _____

Worksheet 29: LINEAR REGRESSION AND STANDARD ERROR OF ESTIMATE

RIDDLE: What's the wacky definition of "kissing?"

Directions: To find the answer to the riddle, write the answers to the problems on the lines. The word in the solution section beside the answer to the first problem is the first word in the answer to the riddle, the word beside the answer to the second problem is the second word, and so on.

You are to *predict D from C*. Round the answers for slope and intercept to two decimal places. Round the standard error of estimate, predicted scores and confidence limits to one decimal place.

C	D
0	5
2	2
2	4
5	8
7	6
8	8
10	12
10	10
11	10

_____ 1. What is the value of the slope?

_____ 2. What is the value of the intercept?

_____ 3. What is the value of the standard error of estimate?

_____ 4. What is the predicted score on D for a subject with an obtained score of 9 on Test C?

_____ 5. What is the upper limit of the 68% confidence interval for the predicted score of the subject in question 4?

CONTINUED

Worksheet 29: Continued

_____ 6. What is the lower limit of the 68% confidence interval for the predicted score of the subject in question 4?

_____ 7. What is the predicted score on D for a subject with an obtained score of 1 on Test C?

_____ 8. What is the upper limit of the 68% confidence interval for the predicted score of the subject in question 7?

_____ 9. What is the lower limit of the 68% confidence interval for the predicted score of the subject in question 7?

SOLUTION SECTION:

2.98 (MOST)   2.0 (DEVISED)   1.09 (LOVE)   -1.74 (ROMANCE)

8.1 (SPOUSE)   0.69 (THE)   5.4 (YET)   -0.6 (HONEYMOON)

10.0 (IS)   1.7 (PLEASANT)   10.9 (OF)   6 (FEELING)

3.7 (GERMS)   1.0 (HAPPY)   7.5 (SPREADING)   9.2 (WAY)

Write the answer to the riddle here, putting one word on each line:

_____ _____ _____ _____ _____ _____

_____ _____ _____

Name: _____ Date: _____

Worksheet 30: DESCRIPTIVE AND CORRELATIONAL CONCEPTS: REVIEW

RIDDLE: What's the worst thing about accidents in the kitchen?

Directions: To find the answer to the riddle, write "T" for "true" or "F" for "false" on the line to the left of each statement. The word at the end of the first true statement is the first word in the answer to the riddle, the word at the end of the second true statement is the second word, and so on.

_____ 1. A frequency polygon is a table in which the first column shows the score intervals and the second column shows the frequencies associated with the intervals. (FOOD)

_____ 2. The median is the type of average that always has 50% of the cases below it. (YOU)

_____ 3. The mean is a measure of variability. (ARE)

_____ 4. The more the scores for a group differ from the mean of the group, the greater the value of the standard deviation. (USUALLY)

_____ 5. In a normal curve, about 34% of the cases lie between the mean and one standard deviation unit above the mean. (HAVE)

_____ 6. A person who obtains a z-score of 0.00 is at the bottom of the norm group. (IS)

_____ 7. A Pearson r of 0.00 indicates that there is no relationship between two variables. (TO)

_____ 8. A Pearson r of -0.95 represents a very strong relationship. (EAT)

_____ 9. A Pearson r's best use is to describe curvilinear relationships. (FREQUENTLY)

_____ 10. The general purpose of linear regression is to develop a straight-line equation that permits the prediction of scores for individuals. (THEM)

_____ 11. The 68% confidence limit for a predicted score yields an interval in which we are certain that the true score lies. (SPOILED)

Write the answer to the riddle here, putting one word on each line:

_____ _____ _____ _____ _____ _____

NOTES:

Dr. P.'s friendly advice: USING A COMPUTER IS GREAT! IT GIVES YOU POWER AND SPEED.

Yet, you still may be getting some wrong answers. If so, here's an important suggestion to help you:

Before doing any assigned work, first do a short, simple problem from your textbook. Most textbook examples have a small number of scores and the results are given.

If you get the same answer as indicated in the text, you know how to use the computer to solve that type of problem. You will also know that the computer program was written correctly. (Yes, even computer programmers sometimes make mistakes.)

Try this technique and write your impressions of it here:

_____

_____

Name: _____ Date: _____

Worksheet 31: PROBABILITY

RIDDLE: What do you get if you cross an elephant with a kangaroo?

Directions: To find the answer to the riddle, write "T" for "true" or "F" for "false" on the line to the left of each statement. The word at the end of the first true statement is the first word in the answer to the riddle, the word at the end of the second true statement is the second word, and so on.

_____ 1. The probability of drawing a king from a deck of 52 cards is 1/52. (ANIMALS)

_____ 2. The probability of drawing an ace from a deck of 52 cards is 4/52. (GREAT)

_____ 3. A probability of 4/52 is equivalent to a probability of 1/13. (BIG)

_____ 4. The probability of drawing a king or queen on a single draw from a deck is 2/13. (HOLES)

_____ 5. The probability of drawing a jack, queen or king on a single draw is 12/13. (JUMPS)

_____ 6. The probability of the occurrence of several mutually exclusive events equals the sum of their separate probabilities. (ALL)

_____ 7. The probability of drawing two aces in a row if the first ace is replaced before the second draw is 2/13. (ZOOS)

_____ 8. The probability of drawing three kings in a row if each draw is replaced before the next is 1/169. (KEEP)

_____ 9. The probability of the successive occurrence of several independent events equals the product of their separate probabilities. (OVER)

_____ 10. The probability of drawing a king followed by a queen in two successive draws if the king is NOT replaced before the second draw is 4/676. (CURIOUS)

_____ 11. The probability of drawing a king followed by a queen and followed by a jack without replacement is 8/16575. (AUSTRALIA)

Write the answer to the riddle here, putting one word on each line:

_____ _____ _____ _____ _____ _____

NOTES:

Dr. P.'s friendly advice: YOU'RE A CHAMPION IN STATISTICS? CONGRATULATIONS!

You can get even more out of the course if you help someone who is struggling. As you explain concepts and procedures, they will become even clearer to you and more firmly entrenched in your mind. You'll also build speed because you'll be reviewing while tutoring. (Also, many people find it more fun to review this way rather than study silently by themselves.)

Identify someone who is having problems in statistics and offer a hand. Remember that he or she may be shy or embarrassed, so you should make the offer. You don't need to offer to be a tutor for the duration of the course. It's O.K. to offer to help with a specific type of computation or concept.

Right after you try this the first time, answer the following questions:

What specific help did you offer? _____

How much time did you spend? _____

Did the other student seem to benefit? _____

Did you benefit? How? _____

Name: _____   Date: _____

Worksheet 32: SAMPLING CONCEPTS

RIDDLE: How can you tell if you talk too much?

Directions: To find the answer to the riddle, write "T" for "true" or "F" for "false" on the line to the left of each statement. The word at the end of the first true statement is the first word in the answer to the riddle, the word at the end of the second true statement is the second word, and so on.

_____ 1. By drawing a simple random sample, one is assured of freedom from sampling errors. (LISTEN)

_____ 2. Using volunteers as the subjects in a study is an example of simple random sampling from the population to which the volunteers belong. (TO)

_____ 3. In simple random sampling, each individual in a population has an equal chance of being drawn. (CHECK)

_____ 4. Using students you happen to meet on campus as a sample of all students on campus is an example of biased sampling. (TO)

_____ 5. If one draws a simple random sample, one is assured of freedom from bias in sampling. (SEE)

_____ 6. The effects of a serious bias in sampling can be overcome by using a very large sample. (TALK)

_____ 7. In stratified random sampling, individuals are drawn at random separately from each stratum. (IF)

_____ 8. Simple random sampling is generally considered to be far superior to stratified random sampling. (HEAR)

_____ 9. The process of dividing a population into strata for the purpose of stratified random sampling introduces bias into the sampling process. (THEM)

_____ 10. The primary reasons for using biased sampling techniques are convenience and economy. (YOUR)

_____ 11. A table of random numbers can be used to draw an unbiased sample only if one can first identify all members of the population of interest. (TONGUE)

_____ 12. An "accidental" sample is an example of a probability sample. (SPEECH)

_____ 13. Stratified random sampling is usually more precise than simple random sampling. (IS)

_____ 14. Using listed telephone numbers as a basis for selecting a sample will yield a biased sample of the population of all residents in a city. (TANNED)

Write the answer to the riddle here, putting one word on each line:

_____ _____ _____ _____ _____ _____

_____ _____

NOTES:

Dr. P.'s friendly advice: PAYING ATTENTION TO FRACTIONS AND RATIOS CAN HELP UNLOCK THE MEANING OF STATISTICS.

Obviously, 1/10 is larger than 1/100. If the numerator is held constant, as the denominator increases, the value of the fraction decreases. Yet, some students fail to apply such knowledge when thinking about statistics. For example, consider the formula for the standard error of the mean. The denominator is the square root of N. Thus, as N increases, the standard error of the mean decreases. The practical implication is, of course, that increasing sample size decreases sampling error.

Consider the numerator. As it increases for a given denominator, the value of the fraction increases. For example, 5/10 is greater than 1/10. Using this principle, state the relationship between the size of the standard deviation and the value of the standard error of the mean:

_____

You will encounter other fractions and ratios in statistics. Don't just learn the formulas mechanically. Pause and, using your knowledge of fractions, think about what they mean.

Name: _____ Date:_____

Worksheet 33: STANDARD ERROR OF THE MEAN

RIDDLE: Why did the elderly man bury his money?

Directions: To find the answer to the riddle, write the answers to the problems on the lines. The word in the solution section beside the answer to the first problem is the first word in the answer to the riddle, the word beside the answer to the second problem is the second word, and so on.

For each item, calculate the standard error of the mean. Round answers to one decimal place.

_____ 1. M = 50.00, s = 12.00, and N = 16

_____ 2. M = 50.00, s = 12.00, and N = 64

_____ 3. M = 50.00, s = 8.00, and N = 64

_____ 4. M = 100.00, s = 30.42, and N = 144

_____ 5. M = 100.00, s = 3.19, and N = 144

_____ 6. M = 100.00, s = 30.42, and N = 7

_____ 7. M = 100.00, s = 50.59, and N = 3

_____ 8. M = 500.00, s = 100.00, and N = 400

_____ 9. M = 500.00, s = 50.00, and N = 167

_____ 10. M = 500.00, s = 50.00, and N = 25

_____ 11. M = 500.00, s = 40.00, and N = 25

SOLUTION SECTION:

8.0 (AHEAD)	51.5 (IS)	9.0 (DEATH)	3.0 (BECAUSE)
10.0 (IT)	3.9 (SENT)	16.9 (HEAVEN)	51.0 (GRAVE)
5.0 (HE)	29.2 (HIM)	6.0 (LIFELESS)	11.5 (WITH)
1.0 (COULDN'T)	1.5 (HE)	0.3 (IT)	2.5 (TAKE)

Write the answer to the riddle here, putting one word on each line:

_____ _____ _____ _____ _____ _____

_____ _____ _____ _____ _____

NOTES:

Dr. P.'s friendly advice: SPEAK UP IN CLASS!

   Some students report that they feel so lost during some lectures that they don't know what to ask; they don't know how to formulate a specific question.
   How to prevent this from happening to you? Ask for clarification as soon as possible after a point is made that you do not understand. Remember that statistics is cumulative. A point you do not understand may be used in developing the next concept.
   You may not have time to formulate a complete, formal question, so it's O.K. to simply say, "Would you explain that again?" (Of course, you need to exercise some judgment as to when and how frequently to interrupt a lecture.)
   Often average and above average students ask most of the questions. If you're a student who seldom or never asks questions in class, do so the next time you don't understand something and record your reactions here:

What did you ask? _____

Did you feel foolish? _____ (If yes, you need to practice asking more questions. The more you do it, the more comfortable you'll feel.)

Name: _____ Date: _____

Worksheet 34: CONFIDENCE INTERVAL FOR THE MEAN: LARGE N

RIDDLE: What do you call a person in a plane when all the engines go dead?

Directions: To find the answer to the riddle, write the answers to the problems on the lines. The letter in the solution section beside the answer to the first problem is the first letter in the answer to the riddle, the letter beside the answer to the second problem is the second letter, and so on.

Since the samples underlying the statistics shown below are large, use 1.96 and 2.58 as the multipliers for computing the 95% and 99% confidence intervals, respectively. Round answers to one decimal place.

_____ 1. If the mean equals 50.00 and the standard error of the mean equals 2.18, what is the upper limit of the 68% confidence interval?

_____ 2. What is the lower limit of the 68% confidence interval associated with question 1?

_____ 3. What is the upper limit of the 95% confidence interval for the mean given in question 1?

_____ 4. What is the lower limit of the 95% confidence interval for the mean given in question 1?

_____ 5. If the mean equals 92.54 and the standard error of the mean equals 4.74, what is the upper limit of the 95% confidence interval?

_____ 6. What is the lower limit of the 95% confidence interval associated with question 5?

_____ 7. What is the upper limit of the 99% confidence interval for the mean given in question 5?

_____ 8. What is the lower limit of the 99% confidence interval for the mean given in question 5?

SOLUTION SECTION:

83.2 (V)	101.8 (I)	97.3 (B)	87.8 (C)	55.6 (F)
80.3 (R)	104.8 (E)	44.4 (X)	4.3 (W)	45.7 (D)
54.3 (Y)	12.2 (Z)	9.3 (J)	52.2 (S)	47.8 (K)

Write the answer to the riddle here, putting one letter on each line:

_____ _____ _____ _____ _____ _____ _____ _____

NOTES:

Dr. P.'s friendly advice: HAVING TROUBLE? MAKE AN APPOINTMENT TO TALK WITH YOUR PROFESSOR OR VISIT DURING WALK-IN OFFICE HOURS.

Many students don't do this because they are shy or simply don't know the protocol for an office visit. If you feel that way, the following may help you. Before you meet with your professor, examine this checklist. Be sure to check off all items before your visit:

_____ 1. You have specific questions and have written them down. (If they are written, you will feel more confident and you won't forget to ask some of them.)

_____ 2. You can easily locate the material on which you have questions because you've noted where it is located.

_____ 3. You've already read the material related to your questions and have given it your best shot.

If you've done all three things on the checklist, there's no reason to be shy or anxious; you're prepared for an office visit.

Your professor is a professional, willing and able to help you.

Name: _____   Date: _____

Worksheet 35: CONFIDENCE INTERVAL FOR THE MEAN: SMALL N

RIDDLE: Why is it NOT true that ants are the busiest animals?

Directions: To find the answer to the riddle, write the answers to the problems on the lines. The word in the solution section beside the answer to the first problem is the first word in the answer to the riddle, the word beside the answer to the second problem is the second word, and so on.
   Look up the multipliers for computing the 95% and 99% confidence intervals in the t table using df = N - 1. Round answers to one decimal place.

_____ 1. If the mean equals 35.20, the standard error of the mean equals 3.97, and N equals 16, what is the upper limit of the 95% confidence interval?

_____ 2. What is the lower limit of the 95% confidence interval associated with question 1?

_____ 3. What is the upper limit of the 99% confidence interval for the mean in question 1?

_____ 4. What is the lower limit of the 99% confidence interval for the mean in question 1?

_____ 5. If the mean equals 49.74, the standard error of the mean equals 2.84, and N equals 6, what is the upper limit of the 95% confidence interval?

_____ 6. What is the lower limit of the 95% confidence interval associated with question 5?

_____ 7. What is the upper limit of the 99% confidence interval for the mean in question 5?

_____ 8. What is the lower limit of the 99% confidence interval for the mean in question 5?

SOLUTION SECTION:

26.7 (ALWAYS)	43.0 (WORK)	38.3 (PICNICS)	27.4 (PLAY)
54.8 (INSECTS)	61.2 (TO)	23.5 (TIME)	43.7 (THEY)
46.9 (HAVE)	42.4 (GO)	44.7 (CRAWL)	31.2 (EVENTUALLY)
39.2 (IS)	57.0 (TO)	52.6 (PLAYFUL)	50.0 (EAT)

Write the answer to the riddle here, putting one word on each line:

_____ _____ _____ _____ _____ _____

_____ _____

NOTES:

Dr. P.'s friendly advice: DIFFERENT FIELDS OF STUDY HAVE DIFFERENT DEGREES OF STRUCTURE AND SEQUENCE.

Beginning instruction in most fields is structured and has a definite sequence. Failing to follow the structure and sequence, however, has varying consequences, depending upon the field.

Suppose, for example, in a survey course on world literature, you fail to read the excerpts from Shakespeare. Chances are good that you can move on to the next assignment and still be able to understand it.

Let's suppose you miss the lecture in statistics that introduces inferential statistics and you fail to read the related material. For the rest of the course, your instructor will talk about the "null hypothesis," "probabilities," and "statistical significance." Unless you go back and learn the material you missed, you will probably be lost.

Name another field of study that is highly structured and has a definite sequence like statistics:

_____

Name: _____   Date: _____

Worksheet 36: NULL HYPOTHESIS AND TYPES OF ERRORS

RIDDLE: What did the optician's daughter do at the party?

Directions: To find the answer to the riddle, write "T" for "true" or "F" for "false" on the line to the left of each statement. The word at the end of the first true statement is the first word in the answer to the riddle, the word at the end of the second true statement is the second word, and so on.

_____ 1. The null hypothesis attributes the observed difference between two means to bias in sampling, i.e., it says that biased sampling created the apparent difference. (WHEN)

_____ 2. If the .05 level is used, there are, on the average, 5 or fewer chances in 100 of making a Type I error. (SHE)

_____ 3. If the .001 level is used, there are, on the average, 1 or fewer chances in 1,000 of making a Type II error. (WENT)

_____ 4. Rejecting the null hypothesis when it is actually true in the population is called a Type I error. (MADE)

_____ 5. Rejecting the null hypothesis when it is actually true in the population is called a Type II error. (ALL)

_____ 6. The level of significance indicates the probability of making a Type I error. (A)

_____ 7. The .50 level is frequently used when conducting tests of significance. (FRIENDS)

_____ 8. If the null hypothesis is rejected, one can be certain that the alternate or research hypothesis is true. (DRINK)

_____ 9. The .01 level is a higher level of significance than the .05 level. (SPECTACLE)

_____ 10. As the probability of making a Type I error is reduced, the probability of making a Type II error is increased. (OF)

_____ 11. Significance testing makes it possible to make absolute, definite interpretations of the outcomes of a study. (THEM)

_____ 12. Significance testing is always subject to some degree of error. (HERSELF)

Write the answer to the riddle here, putting one word on each line:

_____ _____ _____ _____ _____ _____

It's the little extras that make the *BIG DIFFERENCE.*

Dr. P.'s friendly advice: THE ABOVE IS ABSOLUTELY TRUE!

None of my suggestions, *by themselves,* will make you a successful student in statistics. However, the cumulative effect of trying and adapting as many as possible to your study of statistics will make a noticeable difference.

Which of my suggestions have you tried recently?

_____

What were the results?

_____

_____

Name: _____ Date: _____

Worksheet 37: z TEST: POPULATION MEAN KNOWN

RIDDLE: Why did the psychiatrist work in a watch repair shop?

Directions: To find the answer to the riddle, write "T" for "true" or "F" for "false" on the line to the left of each statement. The word at the end of the first true statement is the first word in the answer to the riddle, the word at the end of the second true statement is the second word, and so on.
   The questions refer to a two-tailed (nondirectional) test based on this information:

> The population mean is 100.0 and the standard
> deviation is 15.00. A sample of 36 students
> was tested and obtained a mean of 105.57.

_____ 1. The observed difference between the means is 5.57. (TO)

_____ 2. The null hypothesis states that the true difference between the means is 5.57 (BEGIN)

_____ 3. The standard error of the mean for the z test is 2.5. (PSYCHOANALYZE)

_____ 4. The observed value of z for the difference between the means is 3.58. (USING)

_____ 5. The observed value of z for the difference between the means is 2.23. (ALL)

_____ 6. The observed value of z for the difference between the means is 5.57. (THEM)

_____ 7. The null hypothesis may be rejected at the .05 level. (THE)

_____ 8. The difference between the means is significant at the .05 level. (CUCKOO)

_____ 9. The null hypothesis may be rejected at the .01 level. (PEOPLE)

_____ 10. The difference between the means is significant at the .01 level. (ARE)

_____ 11. To say that the difference between means is significant at a given level is equivalent to saying that the null hypothesis has been rejected at that level. (CLOCKS)

Write the answer to the riddle here, putting one word on each line:

_____ _____ _____ _____ _____ _____

Dr. P.'s friendly advice: NOT GETTING THE MOST OUT OF YOUR TEXTBOOK?

Here are some techniques that work:

1. When reading a chapter, first skim to learn its organization. Note the headings and subheadings.

2. Second, read the introduction to the chapter and summary, if any.

    (The first two steps are called "pre-reading.")

3. Read for details.

Here's an additional tip on reading your textbook:

When you encounter something you don't immediately understand (and that's NOT uncommon in statistics), make a note in the margin and continue reading. Don't stop reading just because you don't understand something. When you get to the end of the chapter, you'll have a better understanding of the entire context. This will help when you go back to the more difficult parts.

Try pre-reading when you read the next chapter in your textbook and write your personal evaluation of the technique here:

_____

Name: _____ Date: _____

Worksheet 38: t TEST: INDEPENDENT DATA: I

RIDDLE: What do foolish shoppers do at Christmas?

Directions: To find the answer to the riddle, write the answers to the problems on the lines. The word in the solution section beside the answer to the first problem is the first word in the answer to the riddle, the word beside the answer to the second problem is the second word, and so on. (Note: The answer to question 9 is a word--"yes" or "no." Both words are given as possible answers in the solution section.)

The scores are for two independent groups.

Group A	Group B
10	6
5	9
7	4
8	9
9	8
10	7
9	

_____ 1. To three decimal places, what is the value of the mean for Group A?

_____ 2. To three decimal places, what is the value of the mean for Group B?

_____ 3. What is the value of the difference between the means?

_____ 4. To two decimal places what is the value of t?

_____ 5. What is the value of the degrees of freedom?

_____ 6. What is the critical value of t at the .05 level for a two-tailed test?

CONTINUED

_____ 7. What is the critical value of t at the .01 level for a two-tailed test?

_____ 8. What is the critical value of t at the .001 level for a two-tailed test?

_____ 9. Is the difference between the means significant at the .05 level (two-tailed)?

SOLUTION SECTION:

8.286 (THEY)	13 (SHOP)	9 (CHEER)	5.07 (SALES)
No (MONEY)	Yes (TREE)	7.1667 (BUY)	4.437 (YEAR'S)
3.106 (NEXT)	2.201 (WITH)	11 (PRESENTS)	1.119 (THIS)
1.08 (YEAR'S)	7.167 (BUY)	1.037 (SANTA)	9.28 (IS)

Write the answer to the riddle here, putting one word on each line:

_____ _____ _____ _____ _____ _____

_____ _____ _____

Name: _____   Date: _____

Worksheet 39: t TEST: INTERPRETATION

RIDDLE: One son went to sea. The other became Vice President of the U.S. What happened to both of them?

Directions: To find the answer to the riddle, write "T" for "true" or "F" for "false" on the line to the left of each statement. The word at the end of the first true statement is the first word in the answer to the riddle, the word at the end of the second true statement is the second word, and so on.

The following questions are based on this information:

Two random samples were independently drawn to form experimental and control groups. The dependent variable was measured and the value of t for the difference between the means was computed to be 2.536. There were 10 subjects in one group and 9 in the other. The investigator wishes to use a two-tailed test.

_____   1.   The difference between the means is significant at the .05 level. (NEITHER)
_____   2.   The difference between the means is significant at the .01 level. (BOTH)
_____   3.   The null hypothesis may be rejected at the .05 level. (HAS)
_____   4.   The null hypothesis may be rejected at the .01 level. (OF)
_____   5.   The .05 level represents a higher level of significance than the .01 level represents. (THE)
_____   6.   At the .05 level, one may be certain that the experimental treatment is effective. (SONS)
_____   7.   Odds are greater than 1 in 100 that random errors account for the difference. (BEEN)
_____   8.   At the .01 level, one can be certain that the null hypothesis is correct. (WENT)
_____   9.   Odds are 5 or less in 100 that random errors account for the difference. (HEARD)
_____ 10.   Odds are 5 or more in 100 that random errors account for the difference. (SAILED)
_____ 11.   Even at the .05 level, it is possible that random sampling errors created the difference. (FROM)
_____ 12.   The investigator should select the significance level he or she will use before analysis of the data. (SINCE)
_____ 13.   The t test would have been just as valid or meaningful for this study if the samples had been drawn in a biased manner, yielding superior subjects in the experimental group. (AWAY)

Write the answer to the riddle here, putting one word on each line:

_____   _____   _____   _____   _____   _____

NOTES:

Dr. P.'s friendly advice: MULTIPLE-CHOICE QUESTION:

Select two of these for use in statistics:

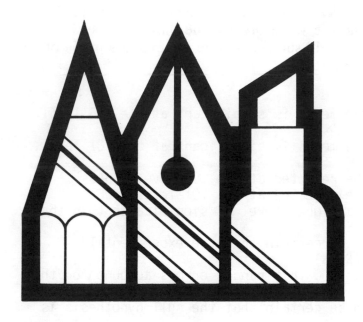

Answer:

    1. A felt-tip highlighter to mark important concepts and formulas in your textbook and notes.

    2. A pencil and eraser so that you can make neat corrections in your notes and computational work. (It amazes Dr. P. that some students come to class eager to learn, yet don't have an essential tool--the humble pencil).

Which of the writing instruments did you take to the last class meeting?

_____

If your list does not include at least two sharp pencils and one highlighter, make a point of bringing the correct tools to the next class meeting.

Name: _____ Date: _____

Worksheet 40: t TEST: INDEPENDENT DATA: II

RIDDLE: Who is the author of the book *Crime Does Not Pay* ?

Directions: To find the answer to the riddle, write the answers to the problems on the lines. The letter in the solution section beside the answer to the first problem is the first letter in the answer to the riddle, the letter beside the answer to the second problem is the second letter, and so on. (Note: The answers to questions 9 and 10 are words--"yes" or "no." Both words are given as possible answers in the solution section.)

   Subtract the smaller mean from the larger mean in your computations. The scores are for two independent groups.

Group C	Group D
19	40
20	34
20	28
25	25
30	38
32	

_____ 1. To three decimal places, what is the value of the mean for Group C?

_____ 2. To three decimal places, what is the value of the mean for Group D?

_____ 3. What is the value of the difference between the means?

_____ 4. To two decimal places, what is the value of t?

_____ 5. What is the value of the degrees of freedom?

_____ 6. What is the critical value of t at the .05 level for a two-tailed test?

CONTINUED

Worksheet 40: Continued

_____ 7. What is the critical value of t at the .01 level for a two-tailed test?

_____ 8. What is the critical value of t at the .001 level for a two-tailed test?

_____ 9. Is the difference between the means significant at the .05 level (two-tailed)?

_____ 10. Is the difference between the means significant at the .01 level (two-tailed)?

SOLUTION SECTION:

11 (H)	24.333 (R)	33.000 (O)	10 (L)	67.333 (Y)
4.781 (N)	Yes (K)	No (S)	1.833 (W)	8.667 (B)
2.39 (I)	9 (N)	27.5000 (G)	3.250 (A)	6 (J)
2.262 (B)	2.201 (X)	29.200 (L)	5.325 (M)	

Write the answer to the riddle here, putting one letter on each line:

____ ____ ____ ____ ____   ____ ____ ____ ____ ____

Name: _____ Date: _____

Worksheet 41: t TEST: INDEPENDENT DATA: III

RIDDLE: You can't escape death or taxes, but how are death and taxes different?

Directions: To find the answer to the riddle, write the answers to the problems on the lines. The word in the solution section beside the answer to the first problem is the first word in the answer to the riddle, the word beside the answer to the second problem is the second word, and so on. (Note: The answers to statistics questions 9 and 10 are words--"yes" or "no." Both words are given as possible answers in the solution section.)
    Subtract the smaller mean from the larger mean in your computations. The scores are for two independent groups.

Group E	Group F
9	5
8	9
0	9
5	7
4	11
4	5
8	15
0	10
9	12
10	14
4	6
5	

_____ 1. To three decimal places, what is the value of the mean for Group E?

_____ 2. To three decimal places, what is the value of the mean for Group D?

_____ 3. What is the value of the difference between the means?

CONTINUED

Worksheet 41: Continued

_____ 4. To two decimal places, what is the value of t?

_____ 5. What is the value of the degrees of freedom?

_____ 6. What is the critical value of t at the .05 level for a two-tailed
test?

_____ 7. What is the critical value of t at the .01 level for a two-tailed
test?

_____ 8. What is the critical value of t at the .001 level for a two-tailed
test?

_____ 9. Can the null hypothesis be rejected at the .05 level (two-tailed)?

_____ 10. Can the null hypothesis be rejected at the .01 level (two-tailed)?

SOLUTION SECTION:

1.72 (UNHAPPY)   5.500 (DEATH)   8.583 (TAXES)   23 (SAINT)

9.364 (DOESN'T)   Yes (OF)   No (CONGRESS)   2.080 (EACH)

21 (WITH)   22 (APRIL)   6.600 (IS)   2.831 (NEW)   10 (AM)

3.819 (SESSION)   2.72 (WORSE)   3.864 (GET)   12 (HELPS)

Write the answer to the riddle here, putting one word on each line:

_____ _____ _____· _____ _____ _____

_____ _____ _____ _____

Name: _____ Date: _____

Worksheet 42: t TEST: DEPENDENT DATA: I

RIDDLE: Detroit has built a new type of car just for big city traffic. What is it?

Directions: To find the answer to the riddle, write the answers to the problems on the lines. The letter in the solution section beside the answer to the first problem is the first letter in the answer to the riddle, the letter beside the answer to the second problem is the second letter, and so on.
    Subtract the smaller mean from the larger mean in your computations.

	Pretest	Posttest
Sam	5	6
Sue	7	8
Sally	8	10
Paul	9	16
Cindy	12	12

_____ 1. To four decimal places, what is the value of the mean on the pretest?

_____ 2. To four decimal places, what is the value of the mean on the posttest?

_____ 3. To four decimal places, what is the value of the difference between the means?

_____ 4. To three decimal places, what is the value of t?

_____ 5. For computing the degrees of freedom, what is the value of N?

_____ 6. What is the value of the degrees of freedom?

_____ 7. What is the critical value of t at the .05 level for a two-tailed test?

CONTINUED

Worksheet 42: Continued

_____ 8. What is the critical value of t at the .01 level for a two-tailed test?

_____ 9. What is the critical value of t at the .001 level for a two-tailed test?

_____ 10. Is the difference between the means significant at the .05 level (two-tailed)?

SOLUTION SECTION:

8.2000 (S)	3.2000 (V)	10.4000 (T)	121 (B)	8.610 (R)
2.2000 (A)	1.241 (P)	30.800 (J)	1.773 (T)	2.776 (N)
5 (I)	No (Y)	3.355 (U)	10 (K)	8 (L)	4.604 (A)
2.132 (Q)	Yes (E)	4 (O)	7 (X)	7.0040 (C)	20 (U)

Write the answer to the riddle here, putting one letter on each line:

A _____ _____ _____ _____ _____ _____ _____ _____ _____ _____ WAGON

Name: _____ Date: _____

Worksheet 43: t TEST: DEPENDENT DATA: II

RIDDLE: Why are the parents of fleas usually unhappy?

Directions: To find the answer to the riddle, write the answers to the problems on the lines. The word in the solution section beside the answer to the first problem is the first word in the answer to the riddle, the word beside the answer to the second problem is the second word, and so on.

Subtract the smaller mean from the larger mean in your computations.

	Pretest	Posttest
Gail	20	25
Bud	21	21
Charlie	19	18
Cynthia	25	24
Jennifer	30	35
Rafe	41	49
Clare	19	26
Jose	20	28
Nick	30	36
Mildred	17	28

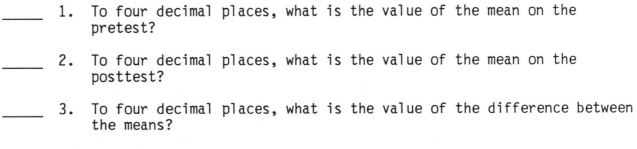

_____ 1. To four decimal places, what is the value of the mean on the pretest?

_____ 2. To four decimal places, what is the value of the mean on the posttest?

_____ 3. To four decimal places, what is the value of the difference between the means?

_____ 4. To three decimal places, what is the value of t?

CONTINUED

Worksheet 43: Continued

_____ 5. For computing df, what is the value of N?

_____ 6. What is the value of the degrees of freedom?

_____ 7. What is the critical value of t at the .05 level for a two-tailed test?

_____ 8. What is the critical value of t at the .01 level for a two-tailed test?

_____ 9. What is the critical value of t at the .001 level for a two-tailed test?

_____ 10. Is the difference between the means significant at the .05 level (two-tailed)?

SOLUTION SECTION:

24.2000 (IT'S)   50 (SCRATCH)   29.0000 (TRAGIC)   8 (FEAR)

1.833 (WILL)   Yes (DOGS)   4.8000 (THAT)   3.650 (THEIR)

4.781 (THE)   3.250 (TO)   2.262 (GO)   2.4000 (JUMPING)

20 (IS)   1.064 (AM)   9 (USUALLY)   10 (CHILDREN)   No (FEVER)

Write the answer to the riddle here, putting one word on each line:

_____ _____ _____ _____ _____ _____

_____ _____ _____ _____

Name: _____ Date: _____

Worksheet 44: t TEST: DEPENDENT DATA: III

RIDDLE: Why did the foolish married man like to drink?

Directions: To find the answer to the riddle, write the answers to the problems on the lines. The word in the solution section beside the answer to the first problem is the first word in the answer to the riddle, the word beside the answer to the second problem is the second word, and so on.

Subtract the smaller mean from the larger mean in your computations.

The scores are from an experiment in which one member of each pair of twins was randomly assigned to a treatment. The other member of the pair was assigned to the other treatment.

Pair	Treatment G	Treatment H
A	2	3
B	5	5
C	0	0
D	7	8
E	4	9
F	7	7
G	6	5
H	4	2
I	9	10
J	8	11
K	3	8
L	2	6
M	5	2
N	7	10

_____ 1. To four decimal places, what is the value of the mean for Treatment G?

CONTINUED

Worksheet 44: Continued

_____ 2. To four decimal places, what is the value of the mean for Treatment
          H?

_____ 3. To four decimal places, what is the value of the difference between
          the means?

_____ 4. To three decimal places, what is the value of t?

_____ 5. For computing df, what is the value of N?

_____ 6. What is the value of the degrees of freedom?

_____ 7. What is the critical value of t at the .05 level for a two-tailed
          test?

_____ 8. What is the critical value of t at the .01 level for a two-tailed
          test?

_____ 9. What is the critical value of t at the .001 level for a two-tailed
          test?

_____ 10. Is the difference between the means significant at the .01 level?

SOLUTION SECTION:

4.9286 (BECAUSE)   No (SINGLE)   15 (DRUNK)   12 (WASN'T)

6.1428 (IT)   1.2142 (USUALLY)   2.779 (DRINK)   13 (SEE)

14 (HIM)   1.827 (MADE)   2.048 (SHE)   2.160 (DOUBLE)

2.2142 (RESTLESS)   3.012 (AND)   4.221 (FEEL)   Yes (HE)

Write the answer to the riddle here, putting one word on each line:

_____ _____ _____ _____ _____ _____

_____ _____ _____ _____

Name: _____ Date: _____

Worksheet 45: SIGNIFICANCE OF THE DIFFERENCE BETWEEN VARIANCES: I

RIDDLE: Statistics show that in 1980 there was an average of 2.4 people in every car on the road; in 1990 it was 1.4. What's the logical conclusion?

Directions: To find the answer to the riddle, write the answers to the problems on the lines. The word in the solution section beside the answer to the first problem is the first word in the answer to the riddle, the word beside the answer to the second problem is the second word, and so on.

Group A: $S = 4.000$, $N = 17$ Group B: $S = 6.000$, $N = 21$

_____ 1. What is the value of the variance for Group A?

_____ 2. What is the value of the variance for Group B?

_____ 3. What is the value of F?

_____ 4. What is the value of the df for Group B?

_____ 5. What is the critical value for the .01 level?

_____ 6. Is the difference significant at the . 01 level?

Group C: $S = 8.127$, $N = 31$ Group D: $S = 5.126$, $N = 41$

_____ 7. What is the value of the variance for Group C?

_____ 8. What is the value of the variance for Group D?

_____ 9. What is the value of F?

_____ 10. May the null hypothesis be rejected at the .05 level?

_____ 11. What decision should be made about the null hypothesis at the .01 level?

SOLUTION SECTION:

16.00 (VERY)   4.00 (AUTOS)   36.00 (SOON)   12.00 (ACCIDENTS)

2.25 (EVERY)   5.00 (ARE)   Yes (BE)   2.51 (WILL)   20 (THIRD)

0.44 (DRIVERS)   Reject it (EMPTY)   3.25 (CAR)   No (ON)

26.28 (ROAD)   Fail to reject (FAMILIES)   66.05 (THE)   15 (AM)

Write the answer to the riddle here, putting one word on each line:

_____ _____ _____ _____ _____ _____

_____ _____ _____ _____ _____

NOTES:

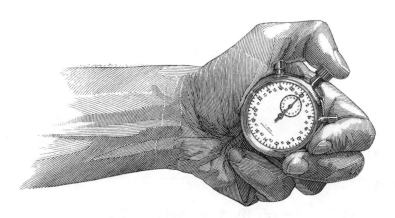

Dr. P.'s friendly advice: MANY TESTS HAVE TIME LIMITS.

Here are three tips for taking timed tests:

1. If you encounter a problem you find very difficult, skip over it temporarily and come back to it later if time permits.

2. If you see that you are running out of time before you've answered all the questions, try to write something for each remaining question--even if you have to jot down a partial, cryptic answer for each. Perhaps you will be able to write enough to get partial credit. No one *ever* got partial credit for a completely unanswered question.

3. Time yourself while doing practice problems for a test. Do a problem on which you are a little slow and record your time here:

Minutes: _____ Seconds: _____

Do several additional practice problems of the same type. Then time yourself again:

Minutes: _____ Seconds: _____

Has your speed improved? _____

Name: _____   Date: _____

Worksheet 46: SIGNIFICANCE OF THE DIFFERENCE BETWEEN VARIANCES: II

RIDDLE: George Washington was "first in war and first in peace." What else was he first in?

Directions: To find the answer to the riddle, write the answers to the problems on the lines. The word in the solution section beside the answer to the first problem is the first word in the answer to the riddle, the word beside the answer to the second problem is the second word, and so on.

Group P: S = 15.593, N = 14   Group Q: S = 16.364, N = 51

_____ 1. What is the value of the variance for Group P?

_____ 2. What is the value of the variance for Group Q?

_____ 3. What is the value of F?

_____ 4. What is the value of the df for Group P?

_____ 5. What is the value of the df for Group Q?

_____ 6. What is the critical value for the .05 level?

_____ 7. Is the difference significant at the .05 level?

Group G: S = 135.521, N = 101   Group H: S = 105.333, N = 81

_____ 8. What is the value of the variance for Group G?

_____ 9. What is the value of the variance for Group H?

_____ 10. What is the value of F?

_____ 11. May the null hypothesis be rejected at the .05 level?

SOLUTION SECTION:

243.14 (FIRST)   267.78 (TO)   12 (DELAWARE)   48 (TREE)

Yes (WEEKEND)   13 (HIS)   1.10 (HAVE)   50 (BIRTHDAY)

2.32 (JUGGLED)   No (TO)   10.26 (RIVER)   1.66 (LONG)

18365.94 (MAKE)   11095.04 (A)   11.64 (REVOLUTION)

Write the answer to the riddle here, putting one word on each line:

_____ _____ _____ _____ _____ _____

_____ _____ _____ _____ _____

NOTES:

Dr. P.'s friendly advice: YOU HAVE A WRONG ANSWER. YOU'VE CHECKED EVERY STEP AND STILL CAN'T FIND THE SOURCE?

It may be time to start over completely fresh. It's sometimes hard to find your own mistakes. Sometimes you "see" what you expect to see, not what is actually there. Maybe you copied part of a formula incorrectly, made a careless error in computation, or gave the wrong command to the computer. Foolish mistakes are sometimes the most difficult to spot--especially when they are your very own foolish mistakes.

If a mistake is truly one of carelessness, it is not likely to be repeated if you start over from the very beginning with a blank piece of paper and a cleared calculator or computer.

For the next few days, record here the types of careless errors you make, if any. (Being aware of the types of errors you tend to make will help you avoid them.)

_____

_____

_____

Name: _____ Date: _____

Worksheet 47: SIGNIFICANCE OF A PEARSON r

RIDDLE: What kind of life does kissing shorten?

Directions: To find the answer to the riddle, write "T" for "true" or "F" for "false" on the line to the left of each statement. The letter at the end of the first true statement is the first letter in the answer to the riddle, the letter at the end of the second true statement is the second letter, and so on.

Study A: r = .492, N = 18

Study B: r = .791, N = 13

Study C: r = .359, N = 20

_____ 1. The df for study A is 17. (L)

_____ 2. The r in Study A is significant at the .05 level. (S)

_____ 3. The r in Study A is significant at the .01 level. (O)

_____ 4. The df for Study B is 11. (I)

_____ 5. The r in Study B is significant at the .001 level. (V)

_____ 6. The null hypothesis in Study B may be rejected at the .001 level. (E)

_____ 7. The r in Study B is significant at the .05 level. (N)

_____ 8. The null hypothesis in Study C cannot be rejected at the .05 level. (G)

_____ 9. The r in Study C is significant at the .05 level. (H)

_____ 10. Because the r in Study C is not significant at the .01 level, it necessarily is not significant at the .001 level. (L)

_____ 11. The null hypotheses for the above tests state that the obtained r's are chance deviations from the population R's of zero. (E)

_____ 12. The null hypotheses for the above tests state that the obtained r's differ from their respective population R's of zero due to bias in sampling. (M)

Write the answer to the riddle here, putting one letter on each line:

_____ _____ _____ _____ _____ _____ LIFE

NOTES:

Dr. P.'s friendly advice: IS THIS HOW YOU FEEL RIGHT AFTER CLASS? IF SO, I'M GLAD; IT SHOWS YOU'VE HAD A GOOD MENTAL WORKOUT.

But before you take that well-deserved break, there's one more thing to do. Review your notes as soon as possible and fill in any gaps. It really will be easier if you do it right away. Fill in what you can from memory and then examine your textbook for the rest. Mark any remaining gaps for discussion with your study group.

As soon as possible after the next class, try this suggestion and record your reactions below. It will probably take less time than you imagine if you do it right after class when the material is still fresh in your mind.

Date: _____   How soon after class: _____

Topic of Lecture: _____

How long did it take to review mentally and examine the textbook? _____

How many gaps remained for discussion with your study group? _____

Name: _____   Date: _____

Worksheet 48: ONE-WAY ANOVA: I

RIDDLE: What did the millionaire want done with her ashes after she was cremated?

Directions: To find the answer to the riddle, write the answers to the problems on the lines. The word in the solution section beside the answer to the first problem is the first word in the answer to the riddle, the word beside the answer to the second problem is the second word, and so on. The scores are for three independent groups.

```
Group A's scores: 3, 0, 5, 2, 1, 7, 3
Group B's scores: 4, 9, 0, 1, 6, 3, 5
Group C's scores: 2, 5, 7, 7, 5, 10, 9
```

_____ 1. What is the value of the mean for Group A?

_____ 2. What is the value of the mean for Group B?

_____ 3. What is the value of the mean for Group C?

_____ 4. What is the value of the between groups (among groups) sum of squares?

_____ 5. What is the value of the within groups sum of squares?

_____ 6. What is the value of the total sum of squares?

_____ 7. What is the value of the between groups (among groups) mean square (variance estimate)?

_____ 8. What is the value of the within groups mean square (variance estimate)?

_____ 9. What is the value of F?

_____ 10. What is the value of the df associated with between groups (among groups)?

_____ 11. What is the value of the df associated with within groups?

_____ 12. Are the differences among the means significant at the .05 level?

SOLUTION SECTION:

18 (IT)   2 (HAVE)   Yes (RICHES)   133.71 (WITH)   8.43 (HELP)

3.00 (SENT)   No (ALL)   2.93 (YOU)   7.43 (NOW)   21.76 (NOTE)

19 (MILLIONS)   4.00 (TO)   6.43 (THE)   43.52 (I.R.S.)   177.24 (A)

Write the answer to the riddle here, putting one word on each line:

_____ _____ _____ _____ _____ _____

_____: "_____ _____ _____ _____ _____"

NOTES:

Dr. P.'s friendly advice: TIME MANAGEMENT PROBLEMS?

Here's an important tip on time management: Make a list of things you need to do. The items on the list should be very specific. "Learn how to use the program to calculate standard scores" is much better than "Do some homework for statistics class." Put the most important item at the top, the next most important item second, etc. For the essential items, make a note of the time and place you will accomplish them.

It's important that the list be in writing. Think of it as a written contract with yourself.

Take a few moments now to list four things you will do in the next 24 hours in their order of importance. Include at least one item relating to this course. Cross off items as you accomplish them.

Item: Time: Place:

1. _____ _____ _____

2. _____ _____ _____

3. _____ _____ _____

4. _____ _____ _____

Name: _____ Date: _____

Worksheet 49: ONE-WAY ANOVA: II

RIDDLE: What's a reliable rule for determining the cost of living?

Directions: To find the answer to the riddle, write the answers to the problems on the lines. The word in the solution section beside the answer to the first problem is the first word in the answer to the riddle, the word beside the answer to the second problem is the second word, and so on. The scores are for three independent groups.

Group D's scores: 3, 1, 5, 0, 2, 0, 1, 1, 2
Group E's scores: 9, 10, 15, 11, 12, 14, 15, 16, 14
Group F's scores: 1, 0, 5, 2, 3, 6, 7, 8, 4

_____ 1. What is the value of the mean for Group D?

_____ 2. What is the value of the mean for Group E?

_____ 3. What is the value of the mean for Group F?

_____ 4. What is the value of the between groups (among groups) sum of squares?

_____ 5. What is the value of the within groups sum of squares?

_____ 6. What is the value of the total sum of squares?

_____ 7. What is the value of the between groups (among groups) mean square (variance estimate)?

_____ 8. What is the value of the within groups mean square (variance estimate)?

_____ 9. What is the value of the F ratio?

_____ 10. What is the value of the df associated with between groups (among groups)?

_____ 11. What is the value of the df associated with within groups?

_____ 12. Are the differences among the means significant at the .01 level?

SOLUTION SECTION:

12.89 (YOUR)	4.00 (INCOME)	3 (INFLATION)	No (YESTERDAY)
Yes (PERCENT)	24 (TEN)	2 (ABOUT)	631.19 (WHATEVER)
1.67 (TAKE)	128.89 (IT)	760.07 (MAY)	58.77 (ADD)
122.21 (IS)	315.59 (BE)	5.37 (AND)	26 (AT)	3 (LOST)

Write the answer to the riddle here, putting one word on each line:

_____ _____ _____, _____ _____ _____

_____, _____ _____ _____ _____ _____

NOTES:

Dr. P.'s friendly advice: GET ORGANIZED!

By now you probably have a lot of material--returned exams and homework, class notes, and scratch paper on which you did calculations. All loose sheets should be three-hole punched and put in a three-ring binder. Usually it's best to put materials on the same topic next to each other--but if you want to file all quizzes separately from all class notes, for example, that's O.K. too. The important thing is to have materials systematically organized, so you can find them when needed.

If you've found yourself frantically searching for something your instructor is referring to--but you can't find it--you need to get organized. While you're searching, you're missing out on the instruction.

If you're not fully organized, make an appointment with yourself to do so as soon as possible.

My appointment to get organized:

Date: _____ Time: _____ Place: _____

Name: _____   Date: _____

Worksheet 50: ONE-WAY ANOVA: III

RIDDLE: Why did the vain man celebrate an anniversary on his birthday?

Directions: To find the answer to the riddle, write the answers to the problems on the lines. The word in the solution section beside the answer to the first problem is the first word in the answer to the riddle, the word beside the answer to the second problem is the second word, and so on. The scores are for four independent groups.

Group G's scores: 5, 6, 6, 5, 4, 1   Group H's scores: 7, 6, 7, 8, 5, 9
Group I's scores: 3, 5, 8, 4, 2, 0   Group J's scores: 9, 9, 10, 12, 8, 12

_____ 1. What is the value of the between groups (among groups) sum of squares?

_____ 2. What is the value of the within groups sum of squares?

_____ 3. What is the value of the total sum of squares?

_____ 4. What is the value of the between groups (among groups) mean square (variance estimate)?

_____ 5. What is the value of the within groups mean square (variance estimate)?

_____ 6. What is the value of the F ratio?

_____ 7. What is the value of the df associated with between groups (among groups)?

_____ 8. What is the value of the df associated with within groups?

_____ 9. Are the differences among the means significant at the .01 level?

SOLUTION SECTION:

20 (TWENTY-NINTH)   3 (HIS)   2 (BEAUTIFUL)   3.94 (ANNIVERSARY)

23 (CAKE)   4.50 (YOUTH)   146.12 (IT)   Yes (BIRTHDAY)   No (HAD)

78.83 (WAS)   224.96 (THE)   1.41 (YESTERDAY)   48.71 (TENTH)

2.73 (FEELING)   1.87 (NEEDS)   12.36 (OF)   10.00 (CANDLES)

Write the answer to the riddle here, putting one word on each line:

_____ _____ _____ _____ _____ _____

_____ _____ _____

NOTES:

Dr. P.'s friendly advice: AVOID THIS FEELING AT FINAL EXAM TIME.

Here's how:

(1) Make a written list of topics you need to study. Do this after reviewing the table of contents in your textbook, the exercises in this workbook and previous tests. Be as specific as possible. "Review how to compute the median" is much better than "Learn about averages."

(2) For each item on your list write a date and time you will do your studying. A number of study sessions lasting a little less than an hour each is better than one very long session.

(3) Plan to meet with your study group or other students to discuss problems at least two weeks in advance of the exam.

Begin now, by writing the date and time for preparing your written list of study topics here:

Date: _____   Time: _____

Name: _____ Date: _____

Worksheet 51: CHI SQUARE: GOODNESS OF FIT

RIDDLE: Why do so many marriages end in failure?

Directions: To find the answer to the riddle, write the answers to the problems on the lines. The word in the solution section beside the answer to the first problem is the first word in the answer to the riddle, the word beside the answer to the second problem is the second word, and so on. Conduct a chi square test for each set of data.

Number of consumers preferring:
Brand A   Brand B   Brand C

50   60   70

_____ 1. What is the value of each expected frequency?

_____ 2. What is the value of chi square?

_____ 3. What is the value of the degrees of freedom?

_____ 4. Is chi square significant at the .01 level?

Number of voters preferring:
Candidate: A   B   C   D

            400   250   190   66

_____ 5. What is the value of each expected frequency?

_____ 6. What is the value of chi square?

_____ 7. What is the value of the degrees of freedom?

_____ 8. May the null hypothesis be rejected at the .05 level?

SOLUTION SECTION:

2 (MANY)   3 (INTO)   4 (DIVORCE)   302 (VOW)   66 (LOVE)

226.50 (PEOPLE)   60 (BECAUSE)   3.33 (SO)   180 (FAILURE)

No (INEXPERIENCED)   0.33 (REJECTION)   254.95 (GO)

0.00 (WEDDINGS)   906 (THIRTY-NINE)   Yes (IT)

Write the answer to the riddle here, putting one word on each line:

_____ _____ _____ _____ _____ _____

_____ _____

NOTES:

Figur	Benenn.
A α	Alpha
B β	Beta
Γ γ	Gamma
Δ δ	Delta
E ε	Epsilon
Z ζ	Zeta
H η	Eta
Θ ϑ	Theta
I ι	Iota
K κ	Kappa
Λ λ	Lambda
M μ	My
N ν	Ny
Ξ ξ	Xi
O ο	Omikron
Π π	Pi
P ϱ	Rho
Σ σ ς	Sigma
T τ	Tau
Y υ	Ypsilon
Φ φ	Phi
X χ	Chi
Ψ ψ	Psi
Ω ω	Oméga

Dr. P.'s friendly advice: STATISTICS WILL ALWAYS LOOK LIKE GREEK TO YOU IF YOU DON'T LEARN THE SYMBOLS.

When you encounter new symbols in statistics, master them right away--otherwise you'll quickly get lost.

By now, you should already know the statistical meanings of several of the Greek letters shown above. Write the meanings of the ones you know here:

_____

_____

Name: _____   Date: _____

Worksheet 52: CHI SQUARE: HOMOGENEITY AND INDEPENDENCE: I

RIDDLE: Statistics show that men who kiss their wives good-bye in the morning live longer. What principle does this prove?

Directions: To find the answer to the riddle, write the answers to the problems on the lines. The word in the solution section beside the answer to the first problem is the first word in the answer to the riddle, the word beside the answer to the second problem is the second word, and so on.

	Medication	No Medication
Improved	50	20
Not Improved	15	40

_____ 1. What is the expected frequency for the upper left-hand cell (row 1, column 1)?

_____ 2. What is the expected frequency for the lower right-hand cell (row 2, column 2)?

_____ 3. What is the value of chi square?

_____ 4. Is chi square significant at the .01 level?

	Choice A	Choice B	Choice C
Men	25	30	32
Women	30	22	19

_____ 5. What is the total number of observations made?

_____ 6. What is the value of chi square?

_____ 7. What is the value of the degrees of freedom?

_____ 8. May the null hypothesis be rejected at the .05 level?

SOLUTION SECTION:

2 (TUCKER)   3.42 (THEY)   33.60 (LOVE)   50 (ARE)   6 (PAIR)

36.4 (MEN)   Yes (UP)   158 (BEFORE)   No (OUT)   26.4 (SHOULD)

31.25 (DEATH)   26.33 (LIVING)   24.06 (PUCKER)   0.40 (NEVER)

Write the answer to the riddle here, putting one word on each line:

_____ _____ _____ _____ _____ _____

_____ _____

NOTES:

Dr. P.'s friendly advice: TIME FLIES WHEN YOU'RE TAKING A TEST.

It isn't enough just to know how to do a problem. Do some extra practice problems before a test to build test-taking speed. Because of your improved speed, you'll have more testing time to check your work and ponder difficult questions.

Here's a checklist to help you decide if you need extra practice. Apply it to each type of problem you might be tested on:

_____ 1. Do you immediately recognize the meaning of each symbol in the formula?

_____ 2. If you are required to memorize formulas, can you write them down quickly and confidently?

_____ 3. Do you know how to begin a problem right away?

_____ 4. For problems that require several steps, are you thoroughly familiar with the sequence of the steps?

Do unassigned end-of-chapter exercises or additional problems in a book you check out of the library until you can check off all four items. (Note: Most introductory books on statistics give the answers to at least some of the end-of-chapter problems.)

Name: _____   Date: _____

Worksheet 53: CHI SQUARE: HOMOGENEITY AND INDEPENDENCE: II

RIDDLE: What would we hear if people only talked about things they really knew?

Directions: To find the answer to the riddle, write "T" for "true" or "F" for "false" on the line to the left of each statement. The letter at the end of the first true statement is the first letter in the answer to the riddle, the letter at the end of the second true statement is the second letter, and so on.

Study 1:

	Sophomores	Juniors	Seniors
Yes	25	30	35
No	16	20	30
Maybe	29	21	15

Study 2:

	Men	Women
Approve	49	62
Disapprove	55	48

Study 3:

	Drug A	Drug B	Drug C
Recovered	15	21	25
Died	20	22	15

_____ 1. The value of chi square for Study 1 is 9.96. (S)
_____ 2. The chi square for Study 1 is significant at the .01 level. (H)
_____ 3. The chi square for Study 1 is significant at the .05 level. (I)
_____ 4. The total number of observations in Study 1 is 201. (E)
_____ 5. The expected frequency for the upper left-hand cell in Study 2 is 53.94. (L)
_____ 6. The value of chi square for Study 2 is 5.43 (A)
_____ 7. The value of chi square for Study 2 is 1.83. (E)
_____ 8. The expected frequency for the upper right-hand cell in Study 2 is 57.06. (N)
_____ 9. The null hypothesis for Study 2 may be rejected at the .05 level. (R)
_____ 10. The value of chi square for Study 3 is 3.11. (C)
_____ 11. One should fail to reject the null hypothesis for Study 3 at the .05 level. (E)

Write the answer to the riddle here, putting one letter on each line:

_____ _____ _____ _____ _____ _____ _____

NOTES:

Dr. P.'s friendly advice: ALMOST ANYONE CAN MAKE GOOD DECISIONS IF HE OR SHE HAS GOOD STATISTICS AND KNOWS HOW TO INTERPRET THEM.

That's the ultimate purpose of statistics--to aid in making decisions. Understanding statistics is necessary if you wish to understand the bases for the decisions being made in many of the fields that affect your daily life.

Make notes below on one or two decisions based on statistics that you may read about in newspapers or magazines during the next week.

_____

_____

Share these notes with your classmates. You'll be amazed at how many different kinds of decisions are being made on the basis of statistics in fields as diverse as government, medicine, business and education.

Name: _____   Date: _____

Worksheet 54: WILCOXON'S MATCHED-PAIRS TEST: I

RIDDLE: What's the wacky definition of "carpet?"

Directions: To find the answer to the riddle, write the answers to the problems on the lines. The word in the solution section beside the answer to the first problem is the first word in the answer to the riddle, the word beside the answer to the second problem is the second word, and so on.

Subtract control group scores from experimental group scores. Rank the differences from low to high.

Pair	Experimental	Control
A	14	12
B	16	12
C	15	15
D	20	13
E	22	19
F	18	15
G	12	11
H	16	18
I	13	17
J	16	20

_____ 1. How many pairs have non-zero differences?

_____ 2. What is the rank of the absolute value of the difference for Pair A?

_____ 3. What is the rank of the absolute value of the difference for Pair B?

_____ 4. What is the sum of the ranks for the positive differences?

_____ 5. What is the sum of the ranks for the negative differences?

CONTINUED

Worksheet 54: Continued

_____ 6. What is the critical value for a two-tailed test at the .05 level?

_____ 7. May we reject the null hypothesis based on a two-tailed test at the .05 level?

_____ 8. Are the results statistically insignificant at the .05 level for a two-tailed test?

SOLUTION SECTION:

6 (IN)   16.5 (RIDING)   10 (FLOOR)   2 (WOOL)   8 (FEET)

No (AN)   26.5 (SHOES)   9 (A)   28.5 (ENJOYS)   20 (WEARS)

Yes (AUTOMOBILE)   17.5 (YARDS)   2.5 (DOG)   7 (WHO)

Write the answer to the riddle here, putting one word on each line:

_____ _____ _____ _____ _____ _____

_____ _____

Name: _____ Date: _____

Worksheet 55: WILCOXON'S MATCHED-PAIRS TEST: Il

RIDDLE: What did the sarcastic parrot reply when asked, "Can you talk?"

Directions: To find the answer to the riddle, write the answers to the problems on the lines. The word in the solution section beside the answer to the first problem is the first word in the answer to the riddle, the word beside the answer to the second problem is the second word, and so on.

Subtract control group scores for experimental group scores. Rank the differences from low to high.

Pair	Experimental	Control
A	20	15
B	30	30
C	33	28
D	35	36
E	29	30
F	25	20
G	15	10
H	16	16
I	38	30
J	30	20
K	33	15
L	19	25
M	20	5

_____ 1. What is the rank of the absolute value of the difference for Pair A?

_____ 2. What is the rank of the absolute value of the difference for Pair D?

CONTINUED

Worksheet 55: Continued

_____ 3. What is the sum of the ranks for the positive differences?

_____ 4. What is the sum of the ranks for the negative differences?

_____ 5. What is the critical value for a two-tailed test at the .05 level?

_____ 6. May we reject the null hypothesis based on a two-tailed test at the .05 level?

_____ 7. May we reject the null hypothesis based on a two-tailed test at the .01 level?

SOLUTION SECTION:

11 (CAN)   4 (WINGS)   2 (CRACKER)   10 (TALK)   Yes (YOU)

No (FLY)   1 (SOAR)   9 (POLLY)   4.5 (SURE)   56 (CAN)

1.5 (I)   64 (DIFFERENCE)   46 (HELPLESS)   13 (AWAY)

Write the answer to the riddle here, putting one word on each line:

_____. _____ _____ _____.

_____ _____ _____?

Name: _____ Date: _____

Worksheet 56: MANN-WHITNEY U TEST: I

RIDDLE: What does the nerd worry about in school?

Directions: To find the answer to the riddle, write "T" for "true" or "F" for "false" on the
line to the left of each statement. The word at the end of the first true statement is the first
word in the answer to the riddle, the word at the end of the second true statement is the
second word, and so on. Rank from low to high.

Study A:

       Experimental Group: 20, 18, 16, 15, 12

       Control Group: 17, 17, 14, 13, 11, 10, 9, 8, 7

Study B:

       Experimental Group: 30, 29, 27, 25, 25, 25, 22

       Control Group: 24, 23, 22, 21, 15, 14, 10, 9, 8, 7

Study C:

       Experimental Group: 50, 49, 46, 40, 39, 37

       Control Group: 50, 50, 43, 42, 40, 38, 36, 35, 33

_____ 1. The rank for a score of 17 in Study A is 11.5. (HE)

_____ 2. The rank for a score of 14 in Study A is 6. (FEELS)

_____ 3. The value of U for the Experimental Group in Study A is 8.00.
       (WORRIES)

_____ 4. The value of U for the Control Group in Study A is 5.89. (SAD)

_____ 5. A two-tailed test at the .05 level for Study A permits rejection of
       the null hypothesis. (THAT)

_____ 6. The value of U for the Experimental Group in Study B is 2.50.
       (ABOUT)

_____ 7. The value of U for the Control Group in Study B is 5.75 (BECAUSE)

_____ 8. A two-tailed test at the .05 level for Study B permits rejection of
       the null hypothesis. (THE)

CONTINUED

_____ 9. A two-tailed test at the .05 level for Study B indicates that the difference is statistically significant. (SHORTAGE)

_____ 10. The value of U for the Experimental Group in Study C is 9.08. (MATH)

_____ 11. The value of U for the Control Group in Study C is 33.50. (OF)

_____ 12. A one-tailed test at the .01 level for Study C permits the rejection of the null hypothesis. (WORK)

_____ 13. A one-tailed test at the .01 level for Study C indicates that the difference is NOT statistically significant. (TEACHERS)

Write the answer to the riddle here, putting one word on each line:

_____ _____ _____ _____ _____

_____ _____

Name: _____ Date: _____

Worksheet 57: MANN-WHITNEY U TEST: II

RIDDLE: What were the last words of the dead magician?

Directions: To find the answer to the riddle, write the answers to the problems on the lines. The word in the solution section beside the answer to the first problem is the first word in the answer to the riddle, the word beside the answer to the second problem is the second word, and so on. Rank from low to high.

Scores for Experimental Group: 50, 48, 47, 44, 43, 40, 40, 39,

36, 34, 30, 29, 27, 26, 22, 21, 20, 19, 17, 16, 15, 12, 10

Scores for Control Group: 46, 42, 40, 38, 28, 26, 25, 14, 12

_____ 1. What is the rank for a score of 50?

_____ 2. What is the rank for a score of 40?

_____ 3. What is the rank for a score of 39?

_____ 4. What is the value of U for the control group?

_____ 5. What is the value of U for the experimental group?

_____ 6. What is the value of Z?

_____ 7. Does a two-tailed test at the .05 level permit rejection of the null hypothesis?

_____ 8. Does a two-tailed test at the .05 level indicate that the results are NOT statistically significant?

SOLUTION SECTION:

0.02 (SAID)   103.00 (SHE)   10 (RABBIT)   8 (ASSISTANTS)

12 (AM)   15 (NEVER)   32 (WITH)   Yes (CADAVER)   24 (HER)

16.52 (HEAVEN)   16.44 (YESTERDAY)   22 (LAST)   13.00 (HELP)

104.00 (BREATH)   No (ABRA)   14.11 (COFFIN)   23 (LIES)

Write the answer to the riddle here, putting one word on each line:

_____ _____ _____ _____ _____ _____,

" _____ _____ "

Dr. P.'s friendly advice: A HEALTHY LIFESTYLE CAN HELP YOU IN STATISTICS.

Good nutrition and regular exercise are great for you. They also will help keep you in good shape for studying statistics.

A small percent of you may feel undue anxiety and stress when working with math and statistics. If you're one, give exercise a try. Take a brisk walk the next time you feel this way and then come back to statistics. You should feel refreshed and less anxious.

When you try this suggestion, write your reactions here:

_____

_____

Name: _____   Date: _____

Worksheet 58: NONPARAMETRIC AND PARAMETRIC TESTS: CONCEPTS

RIDDLE: T.V. is not only replacing radio; it's doing a pretty good job of replacing what else?

Directions: To find the answer to the riddle, write "T" for "true" or "F" for "false" on the line to the left of each statement. The letter at the end of the first true statement is the first letter in the answer to the riddle, the letter at the end of the second true statement is the second letter, and so on.

_____ 1. Nonparametric tests assume that samples are drawn from distributions that are normal. (T)
_____ 2. The t-test is an example of a parametric test. (H)
_____ 3. Wilcoxon's Matched-Pairs Test is an example of a nonparametric test. (O)
_____ 4. For rank data (ordinal data), parametric tests are usually more appropriate than nonparametric ones. (A)
_____ 5. In general, parametric tests are more powerful than nonparametric tests. (M)
_____ 6. The power of a statistical test refers to the probability of rejecting the null hypothesis when it is actually true. (T)
_____ 7. Underlying chi square is the assumption of normality of the distribution in the population. (O)
_____ 8. For nominal (naming) data, one should use a nonparametric test. (E)
_____ 9. Parametric tests are most likely to yield inaccurate results with small samples based on unequal N's that come from distributions that are skewed. (W)
_____ 10. The F test is based upon the assumption of a normal distribution in the population. (O)
_____ 11. Chi square is based upon the assumption of homogeneity of variance. (F)
_____ 12. Even very minor violations of the assumptions underlying the t-test almost always make the test highly inaccurate. (D)
_____ 13. The Mann-Whitney U test is a nonparametric test. (R)
_____ 14. The z-test is a parametric test. (K)

Write the answer to the riddle here, putting one letter on each line:

____ ____ ____ ____ ____ ____ ____ ____

NOTES:

Dr. P.'s friendly advice: THE MESSAGE IS ABOUT THE NEXT TWO WORKSHEETS.

These two worksheets are designed for review, but they are based upon only a sample of the many things you may be expected to know when you take the final exam.

Use these worksheets to jog your memory. If there are answers to some items of which you are uncertain, give these items and related material high priority when you study for the final. As soon as you finish the facing worksheet, write the names of three topics you will give high priority to when studying:

_____

_____

_____

Name: _____ Date: _____

Worksheet 59: COURSE REVIEW: CLASSIFICATION OF STATISTICS

RIDDLE: What happens if you don't pay the exorcist?

Directions: To find the answer to the riddle, write "T" for "true" or "F" for "false" on the line to the left of each statement. The letter at the end of the first true statement is the first letter in the answer to the riddle, the letter at the end of the second true statement is the second letter, and so on.

_____ 1.   The mean is a descriptive statistic. (Y)
_____ 2.   Chi square is a descriptive statistic. (X)
_____ 3.   The median is a measure of variability. (B)
_____ 4.   The range is a measure of variability. (O)
_____ 5.   The correlation coefficient is an inferential statistic. (J)
_____ 6.   The mode is a measure of central tendency. (U)
_____ 7.   The standard deviation is a measure of variability. (G)
_____ 8.   The variance is a measure of variability. (E)
_____ 9.   A single standard score describes a correlation. (K)
_____ 10. The quartile deviation is a descriptive statistic. (T)
_____ 11. The Pearson r is a correlation coefficient. (R)
_____ 12. Spearman's rank-order correlation coefficient is an inferential statistic. (M)
_____ 13. The t-test is a descriptive statistic (N)
_____ 14. The t-test is a parametric test. (E)
_____ 15. Chi square is an inferential statistic. (P)
_____ 16. Chi square is a parametric test. (W)
_____ 17. The Mann-Whitney U is a nonparametric test. (O)
_____ 18. Analysis of Variance is a parametric test. (S)
_____ 19. Analysis of Variance is an inferential statistic. (S)
_____ 20. The Wilcoxon test is a nonparametric test. (E)
_____ 21. Chi square is a correlation coefficient. (F)
_____ 22. The standard deviation is a nonparametric test. (V)
_____ 23. The mode is an average. (S)
_____ 24. The quartile deviation, i.e., semi-interquartile range, is a measure of variability. (S)
_____ 25. The quartile deviation is a test of statistical significance. (I)
_____ 26. The median is a test of statistical significance. (U)
_____ 27. The range is a test of the null hypothesis. (T)
_____ 28. The t-test is a test of the null hypothesis. (E)
_____ 29. Chi square is a test of the null hypothesis. (D)
_____ 30. The median is a correlation coefficient. (Y)

Write the answer to the riddle here, putting one letter on each line:

____ ____ ____   ____ ____ ____

____ ____ ____ ____ ____ ____ ____ ____ ____ ____

NOTES:

Dr. P.'s friendly advice: DO YOU HAVE THE LUCK OF THE IRISH?

Why are some students more successful in statistics than others? Check the one that you think is most important:

_____ 1. Luck/chance

_____ 2. Innate intelligence

_____ 3. Effort/hard work

Research indicates that students who attribute success to "effort/hard work" tend to be the more successful students. Why do you think that this is so?

_____

Name: _____   Date: _____

Worksheet 60: COURSE REVIEW: VOCABULARY

RIDDLE: How do you keep a teenager out of hot water?

Directions: To find the answer to the riddle, write "T" for "true" or "F" for "false" on the line to the left of each statement. The letter at the end of the first true statement is the first letter in the answer to the riddle, the letter at the end of the second true statement is the second letter, and so on.

_____ 1. "N" stands for the number of cases. (P)
_____ 2. "f" stands for frequency. (U)
_____ 3. A "frequency polygon" is a graph. (T)
_____ 4. A "skewed curve" is a symmetrical, bell-shaped curve. (J)
_____ 5. A "centile rank" indicates the percentage of scores that fall above a specific score in a distribution. (E)
_____ 6. A "measure of central tendency" is an average. (D)
_____ 7. The "median" is the point in a distribution that has 50% of the scores on each side of it. (I)
_____ 8. The "mean" is defined as the most frequently occurring score. (T)
_____ 9. The "variance" is defined as the square of the standard deviation. (S)
_____ 10. A "z-score" indicates how far a subject is from the mean expressed in standard deviation units. (H)
_____ 11. A "T score" is a z-score expressed on a scale with a mean of 100 and a standard deviation of 15. (W)
_____ 12. The "intercept" of a line is the point where the line intercepts the Y axis. (E)
_____ 13. The "coefficient of determination" is the square root of the Pearson r. (B)
_____ 14. "Simple random sampling" gives each individual an equal chance of being included in the sample. (S)
_____ 15. The "null hypothesis" is a statement that attributes differences to random sampling errors. (I)
_____ 16. A "Type I" error is accepting the null hypothesis when it is actually false. (L)
_____ 17. "Alpha" is the probability of making a Type I error. (N)
_____ 18. An "inferential statistical test" is a test of the null hypothesis. (I)
_____ 19. "ANOVA" stands for "analysis of variance." (T)
_____ 20. "Nonparametric" tests are tests that assume the underlying distributions are normal. (P)

Write the answer to the riddle here, putting one letter on each line:

____ ____ ____   ____ ____ ____ ____ ____ ____

____ ____ ____   ____ ____

NOTES:

Dr. P.'s friendly advice: YOU'VE SUCCESSFULLY FINISHED THE COURSE. CONGRATULATIONS!

I'm sorry that I wasn't able to provide you with any magic solutions. I hope that you tried many of my suggestions and found a number of them useful. I also hope that you found at least some of my riddles worth an occasional smile.

I'd love to hear from you. Please feel free to write to me with criticisms and suggestions. You'll find my address at the front of this book. I'll respond as soon as possible. Thank you.

Sincerely yours,

Dr. P.

KEY TO ODD-NUMBERED ITEMS

Important Note: If you did not perform the calculations in the manner described at the end of the introduction to this workbook, you may need to make allowances for minor differences when checking your answers.

Worksheet 1: 1. 62, 3. 222, 5. 50, 7. 10, 9. 36, 11. 13, 13. 5, 15. 324, 17. 30

Worksheet 2: 1. 20, 3. -96, 5. -12, 7. 16, 9. -70, 11. -43, 13. 495, 15. -66, 17. -467

Worksheet 3: 1. 10.54, 3. 8, 5. 15.8, 7. 15.9, 9. 8.4

Worksheet 4: 1. 0.02, 3. 0, 5. 13.66, 7. 112.08, 9. 7.16

Worksheet 5: 1. 4/5, 3. 2/9, 5. 4/9, 7. 2, 9. 0.5, 11. 2.67, 13. 2.1, 15. 11/100

Worksheet 6: 1. T, 3. F, 5. T, 7. F, 9. F, 11. F, 13. F

Worksheet 7: (Note: Divide each frequency by 56 and multiply by 100 in order to obtain the percents. If, instead, you use a constant multiplier determined by dividing 1 by 56, you may obtain slightly different answers.) 1. 3, 3. 8.9, 5. 9

Worksheet 8: 1. T, 3. T, 5. T, 7. F, 9. F, 11. T

Worksheet 9: 1. 10.75, 3. 7.00, 5. 15.00, 7. 2.25, 9. 1.00

Worksheet 10: 1. 17.35, 3. 596.71, 5. 57.49

Worksheet 11: 1. 87.5, 3. 51.6, 5. 442.8, 7. 60.9

Worksheet 12: 1. T, 3. F, 5. F, 7. F, 9. T, 11. T, 13. T

Worksheet 13: 1. 12, 3. 11.7, 5. 8.66, 7. 5, 9. 2.0

Worksheet 14: 1. 3.11, 3. 1.11, 5. 11.14

Worksheet 15: 1. T, 3. F, 5. F, 7. T, 9. F, 11. F, 13. T

Worksheet 16: 1. 5.250, 3. 1.05, 5. 29.969, 7. 5.650, 9. 5.60

Worksheet 17: 1. 0.0, 3. -3.3, 5. 1.1, 7. 1.0, 9. 2.2

Worksheet 18: 1. 115.0, 3. 90.0, 5. 100.0, 7. 63.3, 9. 600.0, 11. 350.0

Worksheet 19: 1. 0.4750, 3. 0.4951, 5. 0.1915, 7. 0.4938, 9. 0.1700, 11. 0.4599

Worksheet 20: 1. 0.6826, 3. 0.9902, 5. 0.9544, 7. 0.4987, 9. 0.1359, 11. 0.0215, 13. 0.0188

Worksheet 21: 1. 15.87, 3. 69.15, 5. 50.00, 7. 0.49, 9. 84.13, 11. 30.85

Worksheet 22: 1. 38.8, 3. 14.6, 5. 5.0

Worksheet 23: 1. 0.90, 3. 0.87, 5. -0.78

Worksheet 24: 1. F, 3. T, 5. T, 7. F, 9. F, 11. F, 13. T

Worksheet 25: 1. T, 3. F, 5. T, 7. F, 9. F, 11. F, 13. T

Worksheet 26: 1. 10.5, 3. 5, 5. 1.5, 7. 0.93

Worksheet 27: 1. 0.49, 3. 0.37, 5. 0.25

Worksheet 28: 1. 0.60, 3. 1.2, 5. 0.26, 7. 1.0, 9. 1.5

Worksheet 29: 1. 0.69, 3. 1.72, 5. 10.9, 7. 3.7, 9. 2.0

Worksheet 30: 1. F, 3. F, 5. T, 7. T, 9. F, 11. F

Worksheet 31: 1. F, 3. T, 5. F, 7. F, 9. T, 11. T

Worksheet 32: 1. F, 3. T, 5. T, 7. T, 9. F, 11. T, 13. T

Worksheet 33: 1. 3.0, 3. 1.0, 5. 0.3, 7. 29.2, 9. 3.9, 11. 8.0

Worksheet 34: 1. 52.2, 3. 54.3, 5. 101.8, 7. 104.8

Worksheet 35: 1. 43.7, 3. 46.9, 5. 57.0, 7. 61.2

Worksheet 36: 1. F, 3. F, 5. F, 7. F, 9. T, 11. F

Worksheet 37: 1. T, 3. T, 5. T, 7. T, 9. F, 11. T

Worksheet 38: 1. 8.286, 3. 1.119, 5. 11, 7. 3.106, 9. No

Worksheet 39: 1. T, 3. T, 5. F, 7. T, 9. T, 11. T, 13. F

Worksheet 40: 1. 24.333, 3. 8.667, 5. 9, 7. 3.250, 9. Yes

Worksheet 41: 1. 5.500, 3. 3.864, 5. 21, 7. 2.831, 9. Yes

Worksheet 42: 1. 8.200, 3. 2.200, 5. 5, 7. 2.776, 9. 8.610

Worksheet 43: 1. 24.2000, 3. 4.8000, 5. 10, 7. 2.262, 9. 4.781

Worksheet 44: 1. 4.9286, 3. 1.2142, 5. 14, 7. 2.160, 9. 4.221

Worksheet 45: 1. 16.00, 3. 2.25, 5. 3.25, 7. 66.05, 9. 2.52, 11. Reject it.

Worksheet 46: 1. 243.14, 3. 1.10, 5. 50, 7. No, 9. 11095.04, 11. Yes

Worksheet 47: 1. F, 3. F, 5. F, 7. T, 9. F, 11. T

Worksheet 48: 1. 3.00, 3. 6.43, 5. 133.71, 7. 21.76, 9. 2.93 11. 18

Worksheet 49: 1. 1.67, 3. 4.00, 5. 128.89, 7. 315.59, 9. 58.77, 11. 24

Worksheet 50: 1. 146.12, 3. 224.96, 5. 3.94, 7. 3, 9. Yes

Worksheet 51: 1. 60, 3. 2, 5. 226.50, 7. 3

Worksheet 52: 1. 36.4, 3. 24.06, 5. 158, 7. 2

Worksheet 53: 1. T, 3. T, 5. T, 7. T, 9. F, 11. T

Worksheet 54: 1. 9, 3. 7, 5. 16.5, 7. No

Worksheet 55: 1. 4.5, 3. 56, 5. 11, 7. No

Worksheet 56: 1. T, 3. T, 5. F, 7. F, 9. T, 11. T, 13. T

Worksheet 57: 1. 32, 3. 22, 5. 103.00, 7. No

Worksheet 58: 1. F, 3. T, 5. T, 7. F, 9. T, 11. F, 13. T

Worksheet 59: 1. T, 3. F, 5. F, 7. T, 9. F, 11. T, 13. F, 15. T, 17. T, 19. T, 21. F, 23. T, 25. F, 27. F, 29 T

Worksheet 60: 1. T, 3. T, 5. F, 7. T, 11. F, 13. F, 15. T, 17. T, 19. T

NOTES:

NOTES:

NOTES:

NOTES:

NOTES:

NOTES: